AQA GCSE (9-1)
Biology
Grade 5 Booster Workbook

Heidi Foxford
Shaista Shirazi

William Collins' dream of knowledge for all began with the publication of his first book in 1819. A self-educated mill worker, he not only enriched millions of lives, but also founded a flourishing publishing house. Today, staying true to this spirit, Collins books are packed with inspiration, innovation and practical expertise. They place you at the centre of a world of possibility and give you exactly what you need to explore it.

Collins. Freedom to teach

HarperCollins*Publishers*
The News Building
1 London Bridge Street
London SE1 9GF

**Browse the complete Collins catalogue at
www.collins.co.uk**

First edition 2016

10 9 8 7 6 5 4 3 2 1

© HarperCollins*Publishers* 2016

ISBN 978-00-0819436-9

Collins® is a registered trademark of HarperCollins*Publishers* Limited

www.collins.co.uk

A catalogue record for this book is available from the British Library

Commissioned by Joanna Ramsay
Project managed by Sarah Thomas and Siobhan Brown
Copy edited by Rebecca Ramsden
Proofread by Helen Bleck
Typeset by Jouve India Pvt Ltd
Artwork by Jouve India Pvt Ltd
Cover design by We are Laura and Jouve
Cover image: Shutterstock/Brian Kinney
Printed in Italy by Grafica Veneta S.p.A.

Contents

Introduction

This workbook will help you build your confidence in answering Biology questions for GCSE Biology and GCSE Combined Science.

It gives you practice in using key scientific words, writing longer answers, answering synoptic questions as well as applying knowledge and analysing information.

The questions also cover required practicals, maths skills and synoptic questions – look out for the tags which will help you to identify these questions.

You will find all the different question types in the workbook so you can get plenty of practice in providing short and long answers.

---

2. During clinical trials, new drugs are tested on animals and humans.

What would the new drug have been tested on before animals and humans?

_____ [1 mark]

3. Researchers sometimes use traditional medicines when starting to develop new drugs.

Draw **one** line from each medicine to match it with its correct source.

Heart drug digitalis	Willow trees
Painkiller aspirin	Foxgloves
Antibiotic penicillin	Tree bark
Anti-malarial quinine	Mould

[2 marks]

Monoclonal antibodies

1.
Synoptic
Higher Tier only
Monoclonal antibodies are produced by combining lymphocytes with a particular type of tumour cell. Which type of tumour cell is this? Tick **one** box.

☐ Hybridoma ☐ Lymphocyte
☐ Myeloma ☐ Carcinoma

Remember
Myeloma is a particular kind of tumour and is different from a carcinoma.

[1 mark]

2.
Higher Tier only
Which cells are produced when lymphocytes and myeloma cells combine? Tick **one** box.

☐ Antibodies ☐ Hybridomas
☐ Memory lymphocytes ☐ Platelets

[1 mark]

3.
Higher Tier only
Monoclonal antibodies are used for pregnancy testing.

Give **one** other use of monoclonal antibodies.

_____ [1 mark]

44

Higher Tier content is clearly marked throughout.

Learn how to answer test questions with annotated worked examples.

This will help you develop the skills you need to answer questions.

7

Global warming

1. Which **two** of the following gases contribute to global warming?

| oxygen | carbon dioxide | methane | nitrogen | sulfur dioxide |

[2 marks]

2. The gases that cause global warming occur naturally in the atmosphere, but human activities have increased the level of these gases.

List **two** human activities that have increased the level of these gases.

_____

_____ [2 marks]

3. The graph shows temperature difference compared to 1880 global average temperature between 1880 and 2005.

Describe the pattern shown by the graph. Evaluate to what extent the data provides evidence for global warming. [4 marks]

Worked Example
The graph shows that the temperature has fluctuated but overall there is an increase in global temperature.

The graph clearly shows an overall trend of increasing global temperatures. This is strong evidence that global warming is happening as the temperature increase is more than what has been observed in the past.

Overall, the evidence for global warming shown by the graph is quite strong.

The student has correctly described the general pattern shown by the graph and stated the overall trend.

The student has remembered to make a concluding remark based on the strength of the evidence.

129

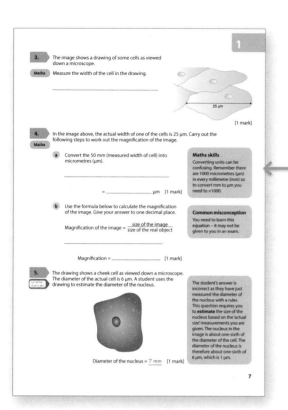

There are lots of hints and tips to help you out. Look out for tips on how to decode command words, key tips for required practicals and maths skills, and common misconceptions.

The amount of support gradually decreases throughout the workbook. As you build your skills you should be able to complete more of the questions yourself.

There are answers to all the questions at the back of the book. You can check your answers yourself or your teacher might tear them out and give them to you later to mark your work.

Plant and animal cells (eukaryotic cells)

1. Draw **one** line from each part of a cell to its correct function.

Nucleus	Where photosynthesis occurs
Chloroplast	Controls what enters and leaves the cell
Cell membrane	Where the cell's activities occur
Cell wall	Controls the cell's activities
Cytoplasm	For support and protection

[5 marks]

2. The diagram shows an animal cell. Complete the labels on the diagram.

[3 marks]

3. Freddie wants to look at an onion cell under a light microscope. He places a thin layer of onion skin on a slide.

Required practical

a Write the letters **A–C** in the correct order to show how he should prepare the slide.

A: Use a paper towel to absorb any liquid that spreads out from under the coverslip.

B: Use a pipette to add a small drop of iodine solution onto the slide.

C: Place a coverslip onto the slide by lowering it carefully from one side.

_____ [1 mark]

b Why does Freddie use iodine solution?

_____ [2 marks]

c State why it is important to 'lower the coverslip carefully from one side'.

_____ [1 mark]

Bacterial cells (prokaryotic cells)

1. Use the words from the box to complete the sentences.

| multi   single   smaller   larger   plants   bacteria   simple   complex |

Prokaryotic cells are _____ and

more _____ than eukaryotic

cells. They are _____

-celled organisms. Prokaryotes include

_____ and archaea.

Literacy
Most scientific words have a Greek or Latin origin which can help you remember the meaning. The prefix 'pro' means 'before' as prokaryotes are the earliest form of life on Earth.

[4 marks]

2. The diagram shows a bacterial cell. Name the parts A, B, C and D.

A: _____

B: _____

C: _____

D: _____ [4 marks]

3. Name the part of the cell where genetic material is found, in

1 prokaryotic cells; _____ [1 mark]

2 eukaryotic cells. _____ [1 mark]

4. *Escherichia coli* is a rod-shaped bacterium. Each bacterium measures approximately 2 μm in length. Convert this figure into mm. Show your workings.

Maths

_____

= _____ mm   [1 mark]

5. Give your answer to question ④ in standard form.

Maths

_____

= _____ mm   [1 mark]

Size of cells and cell parts

1. Owen does some research and finds out the sizes of different cells and organelles. Put the cells and organelles in order of size, from smallest (1) to biggest (5).

Maths

Cells/organelle type	Size	Order (1–5)
Egg cell	0.12 mm	
Sperm cell	40.0 μm	
Ribosome	20 nm	
Nerve cell from giraffe's neck	3 m	
Mitochondrion	2 μm	

[5 marks]

2. Baljit is using a microscope. The magnification of the eyepiece lens is ×10 and the magnification of the objective lens is ×40. What is the total magnification?
Tick **one** box.

Maths

☐ ×40   ☐ ×50   ☐ ×400   ☐ ×4000

[1 mark]

3. The image shows a drawing of some cells as viewed down a microscope.

Maths Measure the width of the cell in the drawing.

_____

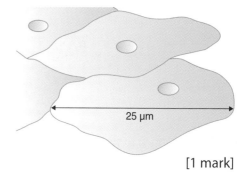

25 μm

[1 mark]

4. In the image above, the actual width of one of the cells is 25 μm. Carry out the following steps to work out the magnification of the image.

Maths

a Convert the 50 mm (measured width of cell) into micrometres (μm).

_____

= _____ μm   [1 mark]

Maths skills

Converting units can be confusing. Remember there are 1000 micrometres (μm) in every millimetre (mm) so to convert mm to μm you need to ×1000.

b Use the formula below to calculate the magnification of the image. Give your answer to one decimal place.

$$\text{Magnification of the image} = \frac{\text{size of the image}}{\text{size of the real object}}$$

_____

Magnification = _____ [1 mark]

Common misconception

You need to learn this equation – it may not be given to you in an exam.

5. The drawing shows a cheek cell as viewed down a microscope. The diameter of the actual cell is 6 μm. A student uses the drawing to estimate the diameter of the nucleus.

 Worked Example

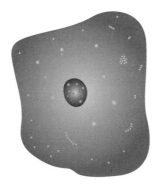

Diameter of the nucleus = 7 mm   [1 mark]

The student's answer is incorrect as they have just measured the diameter of the nucleus with a ruler. This question requires you to **estimate** the size of the nucleus based on the 'actual size' measurements you are given. The nucleus in the image is about one-sixth of the diameter of the cell. The diameter of the nucleus is therefore about one-sixth of 6 μm, which is 1 μm.

The electron microscope

1. Describe what is meant by magnification.

_____ [1 mark]

2. Which of the following is the **best** definition for 'resolution'?
Tick **one** box.

☐ The amount of colour seen in an image.

☐ The smallest distance between two points that can still be seen as two points.

☐ The smallest object that can be observed using a microscope.

☐ The amount by which a microscope can magnify. [1 mark]

3. Explain how electron microscopy has increased our understanding of sub-cellular structures.

_____ [1 mark]

4. Research laboratories often use electron microscopes rather than the light microscopes used in schools. Describe the advantages and disadvantages of using electron microscopes.

_____

_____

_____

_____ [4 marks]

Growing microorganisms

1. Bacteria reproduce by dividing in two. What is this process called? Tick **one** box.

☐ Mitosis   ☐ Meiosis   ☐ Binary fission   ☐ Binary fusion   [1 mark]

2.

Maths

A bacterium has a mean division time of 30 minutes. How many hours would it take to produce 64 bacteria?

_____

= _____ hours   [1 mark]

3.

Required practical

Dot is investigating the ability of two antibiotics to kill *E. coli* bacteria. She spreads the bacteria on two sterilised Petri dishes filled with agar. Then she places a small disc of filter paper containing the antibiotics in the centre of each dish.

a Why is the Petri dish filled with agar?

_____ [1 mark]

b Why are the Petri dishes sterilised first?

_____ [1 mark]

4.

Required practical

The diagram shows Dot's results after 24 hours of incubation.

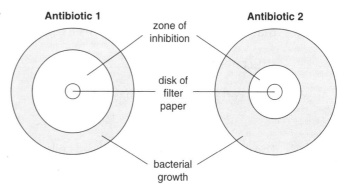

Maths **a** For Antibiotic 2, measure the radius and use it to calculate the area of the zone of inhibition. Write your answers in the table. Use the equation: area = πr^2 ($\pi = 3.14$).

Give your answer to two decimal places.

_____

	Radius (mm)	Area (mm²)
Antibiotic 1 zone of inhibition	11	379.94
Antibiotic 2 zone of inhibition	_____	_____

[2 marks]

b Which antibiotic was **most** effective? Explain why.

_____

_____ [2 marks]

Cell specialisation and differentiation

1. Use words from the box to complete the sentences.

| specialised | unspecialised | differentiate | mutated | cilia |

We start our lives as a single fertilised egg which grows to become an embryo. At this

point the cells are _____, but have the potential to

_____ into any of 200 or so specialised cell types

that make up the human body. As a cell differentiates it develops sub-cellular

structures such as _____ to enable it to carry

out a certain function. It has become a _____ cell. [4 marks]

2. The process of forming specialised cells to make them suitable for their function is called (tick **one** box):

☐ Adaptation

☐ Differentiation

☐ Specialisation

☐ Mitosis [1 mark]

Literacy

Make sure you can explain the difference between key words that are closely linked. Cell differentiation is the process of how a specialised cell is made, whereas cell specialisation is how certain cells are adapted to a function.

3. How are muscle cells adapted to release a lot of energy?

_____

_____ [1 mark]

4. The diagram shows a red blood cell.

Describe and explain how red blood cells are adapted for the efficient uptake and transport of oxygen.

_____

_____

_____

_____

cytoplasm containing
haemoglobin, which
transports oxygen

cell membrane

[4 marks]

Cell division by mitosis

1. Which of the following statements **best** describes mitosis? Tick **one** box.

☐ Mitosis produces two new cells that are identical to each other, and to the parent cell.

☐ Mitosis produces one old cell and one new cell that are identical.

☐ Mitosis produces two new cells that are genetically different.

☐ Mitosis produces some cells that have double the amount of chromosomes. [1 mark]

2. Give the total number of chromosomes you would expect to find in a human cell produced by mitosis.

_____ [1 mark]

3. Draw **one** line from each stage of the cell cycle shown in the diagram to link it with the correct description of the cell cycle in the table.

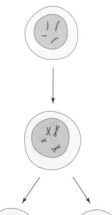

The cytoplasm and membrane divide and two identical cells are formed.

The DNA replicates to form two copies of each chromosome. One set of chromosomes is pulled to each end of the cell and the nucleus divides.

The cell grows. The number of sub-cellular structures, e.g. mitochondria, increases.

4.

A human cell completed the cell cycle in 23 hours 18 minutes.

Maths

a How many cell cycles would be needed to produce eight cells?

_____

Number of cell cycles = _____ [1 mark]

Maths skills

Questions that require you to carry out calculations may ask you to convert units, e.g. from hours to minutes or vice versa. Make sure you read the questions carefully. Underline the units you are asked to answer the question in.

b Calculate the time required in minutes for this cell to produce eight cells.

_____

Time required = _____ minutes [2 marks]

5. In the cell cycle, where are chromosomes found before mitosis starts?

_____ [1 mark]

6. State **two** things that must happen during the cell cycle before mitosis can begin.

_____ [1 mark]

Stem cells

1. Use the words from the box below to complete the sentences.

| embryos children differentiate mutate bone-marrow muscle |

Most cells in your body are differentiated for one particular function, but some are completely unspecialised. These are called stem cells. They can

_____ into many different types of cells when

they are needed. Human stem cells are found in _____

and in some adult tissue such as _____. [3 marks]

2. A human stem cell can develop into what? Tick **one** box.

☐ Gametes ☐ Some cells

☐ Only nerve cells ☐ Any type of human cell [1 mark]

3. Plants also produce stem cells. What is the name of the tissue that produces stem cells in plants?

_____ [1 mark]

4. One way that scientists can investigate stem cells is to use spare embryos from *in-vitro* fertilisation (IVF) treatment. A fertilised egg develops into an embryo and stem cells are removed for research. Give **one** reason why people might object to research on embryonic stem cells.

_____ [1 mark]

5. To avoid ethical issues concerning embryos, stem cells in the future may be taken from which source? Tick **one** box.

☐ Blood ☐ Umbilical cord ☐ Rats ☐ Lungs of an adult [1 mark]

6. Stem cell transplants could help people with paralysis. What type of cell would need to be grown from stem cells to help a person with paralysis?

_____ [1 mark]

7. Evaluate the risks and benefits associated with the use of stem cells for medical treatments. A student's answer to this question is shown below.

Worked Example

I think we should be using stem cells for treatments because it can make people's illness or conditions better and can improve their quality of life. Stem cells can be used to treat and reduce suffering for many conditions like Parkinson's and diabetes or after treatment for cancer. Another benefit is that there is hardly any risk of rejection.

Overall, if a person is ill and can have stem cell treatment, it is better to take the risk because the benefits of a better life would always outweigh the risks.

> The student has correctly outlined the benefits which would have gained 2 marks, but they have not outlined the risks (unknown long term side effects, chance of rejection if stem cells are not from same person). They have lost marks by not writing about what the risks are.

> The student has evaluated the information they have presented and given an overall opinion based on this, so would get a mark for evaluating.

[5 marks]

Diffusion

1. Which of the following statements **best** describes the process of diffusion? Tick **one** box.

Diffusion is the movement of:

☐ molecules from an area of high concentration to an area of low concentration.

☐ molecules from an area of low concentration to an area of high concentration.

☐ gas and water molecules that move randomly.

☐ water molecules that move against a concentration gradient.

[1 mark]

2. The diagram shows a cell surrounded by oxygen. Draw an arrow on the diagram to show which direction the oxygen particles will move in.

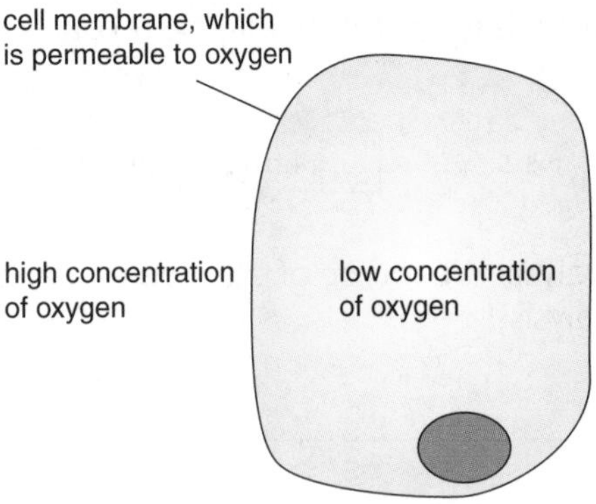

cell membrane, which is permeable to oxygen

high concentration of oxygen

low concentration of oxygen

[1 mark]

3. Name **two** factors that affect the rate of diffusion.

_____

_____ [2 marks]

4. Red blood cells are **not** normally able to diffuse from the blood into the surrounding body tissues, but substances such as oxygen or glucose are. Explain why this is.

_____ [1 mark]

5. Explain why the rate of diffusion of carbon dioxide into stomata on a leaf is higher on a warm day.

_____

_____ [2 marks]

6. Describe and explain the role of diffusion in gas exchange in the lungs.

_____

_____

_____

_____

_____ [6 marks]

Exchange surfaces in animals

1. The surface area of a cell affects the rate at which particles can enter and leave the cell. The table shows different-sized cubes that represent cells. Complete the table by calculating the surface area, volume and surface area to volume ratio (SA:V) for the 3 × 3 × 3 cm cube.

Cubes representing cells (cm)	Surface area (cm²)	Volume (cm³)	SA:V
1 cm cube	6	1	6:1
2 cm cube	24	8	3:1
3 cm cube	_____	_____ _____	

Maths

You need to know how to calculate the surface area to volume ratio. Make sure you learn the formula:

Surface area to volume ratio

$= \dfrac{\text{surface area}}{\text{volume}}$

_____ [3 marks]

2. The diagram shows **two** different single-celled organisms.

A   B

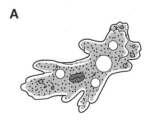
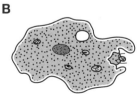

Explain which cell, **A** or **B**, could support a faster rate of diffusion of nutrients.

_____

_____ [2 marks]

3. Single-celled organisms do **not** have lungs, but large multicellular organisms like humans do have lungs. Explain why.

_____

_____

_____

_____ [4 marks]

4. Using the diagram, describe how the surface of the small intestine is adapted for exchanging materials. Explain how it is adapted for this.

The villi

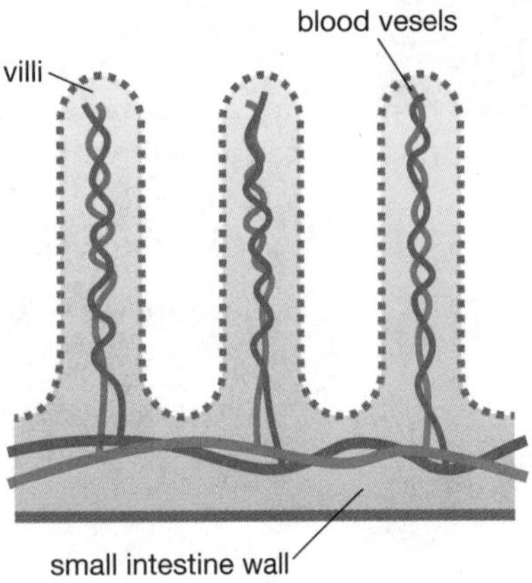

blood vesels

villi

small intestine wall

_____

_____

_____

_____

_____ [3 marks]

Osmosis

1. Use the words from the box to complete the sentences.

concentrated	gas	water	dilute

Osmosis is the movement of _____ molecules from a

_____ solution to a

_____ solution through a partially

permeable membrane. [3 marks]

Literacy

When writing about osmosis, use the word 'concentration'. Students often say that water moves from an area where there is lots of water to an area where there is little water; but this is not correct and will not gain marks.

2. What is meant by a partially permeable membrane?

_____ [1 mark]

3. Tim investigates the effect of different concentrations of sugar solution on the mass of potato tissue. Using a cork borer, he cuts eight equal-sized potato cylinders.

Required practical

He measures and records the mass of each one.

Next, he places each potato cylinder into a boiling tube containing a different concentration of sugar. He leaves them for 45 minutes before removing each one, blotting it dry, then weighing its mass.

Tim calculates the change in mass. He uses this to calculate the percentage change in mass of each cylinder.

a Explain why Tim blotted dry his cylinders.

_____ [1 mark]

b Why were the cylinders left in the sugar solutions for 45 minutes?

_____ [1 mark]

Tim's results are shown below.

Boiling tube number	1	2	3	4	5	6	7	8
Concentration of sugar solution (M)	0.1	0.2	0.3	0.4	0.5	0.6	0.7	0.8
% change in mass of potato cylinder	6.5	5.0	3.0	0.0	−3.5	−5	−7.5	−9.5

Maths **c** Draw a graph to show concentration of sugar solution against percentage change in mass. Add a line of best fit.

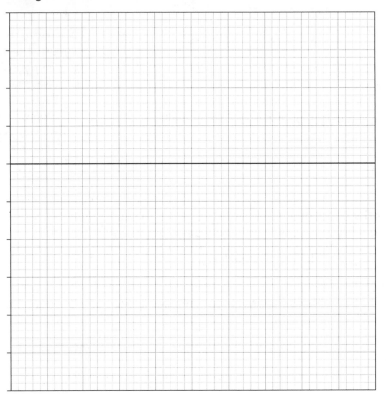

[3 marks]

Maths **d** Use your graph to estimate the percentage change of mass if a 0.9 M concentration of sugar solution is used.

Percentage change = _____ %   [1 mark]

e Tim concludes that the concentration of the sugar solution inside potato cells is about 0.4 M. Do you agree? Explain your answer.

_____

_____   [2 marks]

Active transport

1. Use the words from the box to complete the sentences.

heat	higher	against	along	energy	lower

Active transport is the process by which dissolved molecules move across a cell

membrane from a _____ to a _____

concentration. In active transport, particles move _____
the concentration gradient and therefore require an input of

_____ from the cell.   [4 marks]

2. Active transport allows mineral ions to be absorbed from the soil into the plant root hair cells.

Explain why active transport is necessary for ions to be transported into the root hair cells.

_____

_____   [2 marks]

3. A student is asked to compare active transport and diffusion. Their answer is shown
below.   [4 marks]

Worked Example

Active transport works against a
concentration gradient whereas
diffusion works along a concentration
gradient.

> The command word 'compare' means to
> consider differences and similarities and the
> student has correctly included a similarity to
> gain full marks.

Active transport requires energy from
respiration whereas diffusion does
not require energy. Both are forms of
transport that move substances.

> The student has correctly compared active
> transport and diffusion. Their answer
> contains the right amount of detail and good
> use of scientific language.

Digestive system

1. The diagram shows the human digestive system. Complete the labels using the words below.

| large intestine | oesophagus | small intestine |

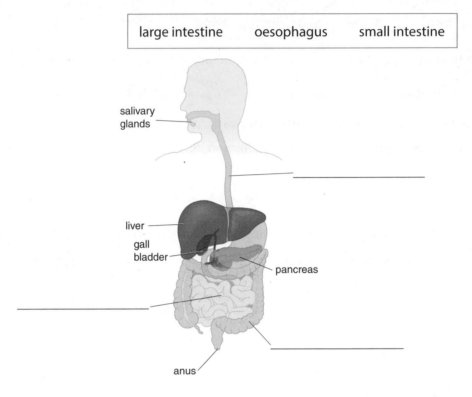

salivary glands

liver

gall bladder

pancreas

anus

[3 marks]

2. Which of the following statements **best** describes the digestive system? Tick **one** box.

☐ An organ system in which several organs work together to break down and absorb food.

☐ An organ consisting of the stomach which digests and absorbs all food.

☐ A tissue that is specialised for absorbing glucose.

☐ All of the above. [1 mark]

3. Why is digestion necessary?

_____ [1 mark]

4. Explain how physical digestion is different from chemical digestion.

_____

_____ [2 marks]

Digestive enzymes

1. Use words from the box to complete the sentences.

| stomach | respiration | bloodstream | large | small | bile salts | proteins |

Digestive enzymes break down food into _____ molecules that can be

absorbed into the _____ . The products of digestion are used to build

new carbohydrates, lipids and _____ . Some of the glucose is used in

_____ .

[4 marks]

2. Complete the table.

Enzyme	Site of production	Reaction
Amylase	_____	Starch to _____
_____	Stomach, pancreas, small intestine	Protein to amino acids
Lipase	Pancreas, small intestine	_____ to fatty acids and glycerol

[4 marks]

3. Draw **one** line from each test to the biological molecules that it identifies.

Benedict's test		Carbohydrates – starch
Biuret test		Carbohydrates – sugars
Iodine test		Proteins
		Lipids

[3 marks]

4.

Required practical

a Joanne conducts three different food tests on peanuts to find out what they contain. First she grinds the nuts with a pestle and mortar before adding distilled water.

Explain why she does this.

_____

_____ [2 marks]

> **Practical**
>
> You could be tested on any of the food tests in the exam. Make sure you know the names of the reagents, how to conduct the test, and the colour change to expect.

b Joanne wants to find out if milk contains protein. Describe a test to find out if protein is present.

_____

_____ [2 marks]

Factors affecting enzymes

1.

Required practical

Sarah investigates the effect of temperature on the activity of the enzyme amylase. She uses a continuous sampling technique to determine the time taken to completely digest a starch solution at a range of temperatures. Every 30 seconds she uses iodine solution to test for starch.

a Describe how Sarah will know when the starch has been broken down.

_____ [1 mark]

b Sarah uses a water bath to heat the amylase. Give **one** advantage of using a water bath rather than a Bunsen burner and beaker of water to heat the amylase.

_____ [1 mark]

c What is meant by a 'continuous sampling technique'?

_____ [1 mark]

d Sarah's results are shown in the graph.

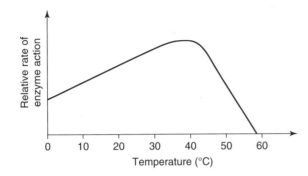

Label the graph to show the optimum temperature for amylase. [1 mark]

e Describe and explain what is happening at this point.

_____

_____

_____ [2 marks]

> **Command words**
>
> Make sure you know the difference between **'describe'** and **'explain'**.
>
> 'Describe' asks you to recall some facts, events or a process in an accurate way.
>
> 'Explain' means you should state reasons for something happening. You need to link points in the answer. Use linking words such as 'so', 'therefore', 'because', 'due to' or 'since'.

Heart and blood vessels

• •

1. The diagram shows a heart.

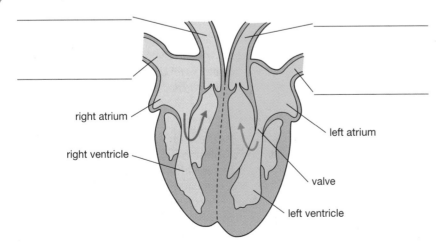

a Add labels to the diagram for the following vessels: aorta, vena cava, pulmonary artery, pulmonary vein. [4 marks]

b Add an arrow to the diagram to show where oxygenated blood from the lungs enters the heart. [1 mark]

c Add an arrow to the diagram to show where oxygenated blood leaves the heart to be pumped around the body. [1 mark]

2. Which of the following statements about pacemakers are true? Tick **two** boxes.

☐ A pacemaker is a group of cells in the right atrium of the heart.

☐ A pacemaker is located in the brain and controls the heart rate.

☐ Artificial pacemakers are used to treat faulty valves in the heart.

☐ Artificial pacemakers can be used to correct irregularities in the heart rate. [2 marks]

3. Give **two** ways in which capillaries are structurally adapted to deliver the maximum amount of oxygen and glucose to respiring cells.

_____

_____ [2 marks]

4. Compare the structure and function of an artery with that of a vein. A student's answer to this question is given below. [6 marks]

Worked Example

The arteries have thicker walls and a smaller hole inside than veins.

Veins have valves.

The arteries carry oxygenated blood away from the heart, whereas the veins carry deoxygenated blood towards the heart (except the pulmonary artery).

The arteries have pressure and a pulse but the veins have none.

Use scientific terminology: 'a smaller lumen' rather than 'a smaller hole' as these are more likely to be on the mark scheme.

Make sure your answers are clear. The word 'none' used at the end of the student answer refers to the pressure and the pulse. It would be better to write 'the veins carry blood under lower pressure and have no pulse'.

The command word 'compare' means you should consider the differences and the similarities. This answer does not contain any similarities (e.g. they both carry blood around the body) so it would not get in the 5–6-mark band.

Blood

1. Complete the table to describe the components of blood and their functions.

Component of blood	Function
Plasma	Transports substances such as hormones, antibodies, glucose, amino acids and waste substances.
Red blood cells	_____.
White blood cells	_____.
_____	Help the clotting process at wound sites.

[3 marks]

2. List **three** substances carried in the plasma.

_____

[3 marks]

3. A blood test shows that a patient has a very high white blood cell count. Suggest a reason for this.

_____

[1 mark]

4. Explain how a biconcave shape helps a red blood cell carry out its function.

_____

_____

[2 marks]

5. **a** Approximately 55% of the blood is plasma. If a person has 6 500 cm³ of blood in their body, how much would be plasma?

Maths

_____

Plasma = _____ cm³   [1 mark]

b In 1 mm³ of blood there are about 5 000 000 red blood cells. Write this number in standard form.

_____

= _____ red blood cells   [1 mark]

Heart–lungs system

1. Which of the following **best** describes the passage of air into the lungs? Tick **one** box.

☐ Bronchus, bronchioles, trachea, alveoli.

☐ Bronchus, bronchioles, alveoli, trachea.

☐ Trachea, bronchiole, bronchus, alveoli.

☐ Trachea, bronchus, bronchiole, alveoli.   [1 mark]

2. Why is a human described as having a double circulatory system?

_____

_____   [2 marks]

3. The diagram shows gas exchange in the alveoli.

Synoptic

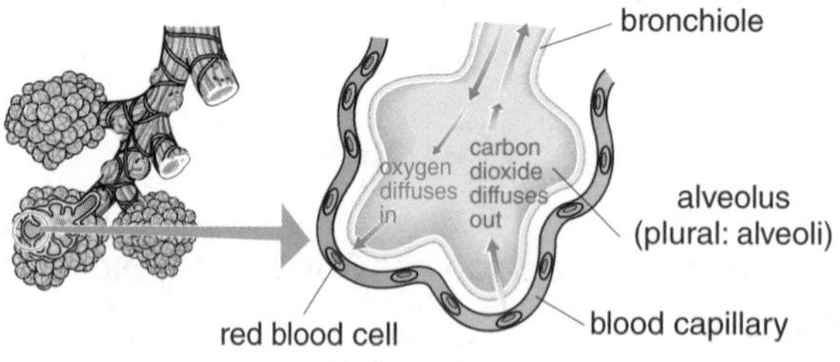

Describe how the alveoli are adapted for efficient diffusion of oxygen and carbon dioxide. Explain how these adaptations help with diffusion.

_____

_____

> **Common misconception**
> Breathing is ventilation, or the movement of air in and out of the lungs. Respiration is **not** the same as breathing. Respiration is the release of energy from glucose, and it takes place in cells.

26

_____

_____ [4 marks]

Coronary heart disease

1. Why is coronary heart disease described as a non-communicable disease?

_____ [1 mark]

2. Write the letters in the correct order to describe the order of events in coronary heart disease.

A	The coronary arteries become narrow.
B	Heart muscle cells become so starved of oxygen that they stop contracting.
C	Layers of fatty material build up inside the coronary arteries.
D	Less oxygen gets to the heart muscle cells around the affected coronary artery.

_____ [4 marks]

3. Faulty heart valves do not open properly or they leak. Explain what effect this might have on the heart.

_____

_____ [2 marks]

4. Artificial valves may be used to replace faulty valves. Give **one** advantage and **one** disadvantage of using an artificial valve to treat a patient with a faulty valve.

Advantage: _____

Disadvantage: _____ [2 marks]

5. Barbara has coronary heart disease. She will have an operation to put a stent in her coronary artery. She will also take statins to control her blood cholesterol levels. Explain how these treatments may prevent a heart attack.

Stent: _____

Statins: _____ [2 marks]

6. Lifestyle changes are recommended for patients having stents, replacement valves or heart transplants. Suggest **two** pieces of lifestyle advice a doctor might give to a patient receiving treatment for cardiovascular disease.

_____

_____ [2 marks]

7. A heart transplant is an operation to replace a damaged heart with a healthy heart from a donor who has recently died. A student was asked to evaluate the benefits and the risks associated with this form of treatment. [5 marks]

Worked Example

The benefits are that with a heart transplant the person will live longer. Also they will have a better quality of life because they will have more energy and strength with a new heart.

> The student has correctly outlined the benefits of a heart transplant.

The risks are that the person has to have surgery which is dangerous if it goes wrong. The person could bleed to death or get an infection from the operation. Also, the person would also have to take anti-rejection drugs which might have side effects.

> The risks have been correctly identified.

Overall, the benefits outweigh the risks because the person will be alive longer with a heart transplant. The person would probably die sooner if they did not have the transplant.

> This answer would gain full marks. The student has understood the question and the command word 'evaluate', which requires weighing up the information to come to a judgement.

1. Which of the following are the biggest risk factors for non-communicable diseases? Tick **one** box.

☐ Exposure to air pollution, unhealthy diet and the harmful use of alcohol.

☐ Tobacco use, malnutrition and exposure to carcinogens.

☐ Tobacco use, physical inactivity, unhealthy diet and the harmful use of alcohol.

☐ Exposure to radiation, harmful intake of caffeine and lack of sleep. [1 mark]

2. Cardiovascular disease is one of the biggest causes of premature death in the UK. Name **three** risk factors for cardiovascular disease.

1 _____

2 _____

3 _____ [3 marks]

3. Suggest why is it difficult to prove that a non-communicable disease is caused by **one** particular factor.

_____

_____ [2 marks]

4.

Maths

The graph shows the number of deaths caused by coronary heart disease for men and women in different age categories. Use the information in the graph to answer the following questions.

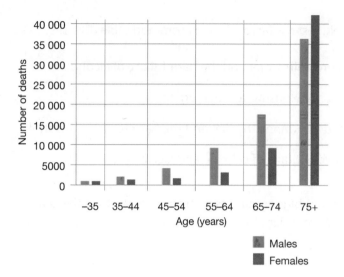

a Approximately how many deaths caused by coronary heart disease occur in the 55–64 age group for females? _____ [1 mark]

b Which of the following statements could be concluded from the data? Tick **one** box.

☐ More males suffer heart attacks than females in every age group.

☐ More older people suffer coronary heart disease than younger people.

☐ Children do not suffer from coronary heart disease.

☐ Men eat more fatty foods than women. [1 mark]

c In most age groups more men than women die of coronary heart disease. Suggest a reason why there are more coronary heart disease deaths in **women aged 75 and above** than for men.

_____ [1 mark]

Cancer

1. Use the words from the box to complete the sentences.

| limited mutation gland tumour catalyst lifestyle strict brain |

Body cells normally divide under _____ control. Sometimes a

_____ causes this control to be lost. When cells divide too often they form a

_____ . This can be a result of things in our _____ or genetic
risk factors. [4 marks]

2. Give **three** risk factors associated with cancer.

_____

_____ [3 marks]

3. Which of the following statements about cancer are true? Tick **two** boxes.

☐ Tumours always start in the brain and then spread to other parts of the body.

☐ Viruses living in cells can be the trigger for certain cancers.

☐ It only takes one mutation in the DNA to trigger cancer.

☐ As a tumour grows, cancer cells can detach and spread to other parts of the body.

☐ All tumours are cancerous. [2 marks]

4. What is a carcinogen?

_____ [1 mark]

5. Describe **two** differences between a benign and a malignant tumour.

_____

_____

_____ [2 marks]

Leaves as plant organs

1. The diagram shows the internal structure of a leaf. Use words from the box to label the diagram.

| palisade cell | spongy mesophyll cell | stoma | guard cell | chlorophyll |
| vacuole | xylem | | meristem tissue | |

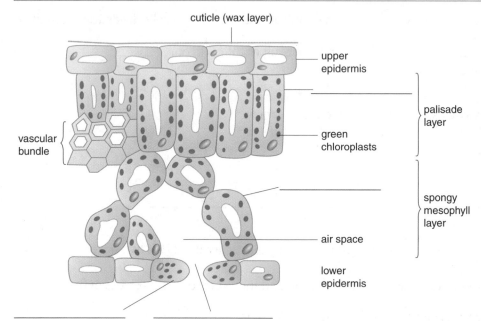

cuticle (wax layer)

upper epidermis

palisade layer

vascular bundle

green chloroplasts

spongy mesophyll layer

air space

lower epidermis

[4 marks]

2. Why is the leaf described as a plant 'organ'?

_____ [1 mark]

3. Name **two** structures found in the vascular bundles.

_____ [2 marks]

Remember

You will be expected to know the difference between a cell, tissue, organ and organ system. Make sure you are clear on how they are different and how they are linked.

4. Which statement **best** describes where meristem tissue is found? Tick **one** box. [1 mark]

☐ The roots and shoots of a plant. ☐ The roots of a plant.

☐ The shoots of a plant. ☐ The xylem and phloem.

5. Leaves are adapted for capturing light for photosynthesis. Explain how the following structures are adapted to collect light.

Broad leaves: _____

Palisade cells: _____

Thin and transparent upper epidermis: _____ [3 marks]

Transpiration

1. Circle **three** factors in the box that affect the rate of transpiration.

| light intensity   carbon dioxide concentration   length of roots   temperature   wind |

[3 marks]

2. Which of the following statements **best** describes transpiration? Tick **one** box.

☐ The evaporation of water from the leaf.

☐ The absorption of water from the soil into the roots.

☐ The movement of dissolved sugars around the plant.

☐ The movement of water through the plant and leaves. [1 mark]

3.

Maths

Ben investigates the rate of water loss from a plant shoot using a potometer. He sets up the equipment as shown.

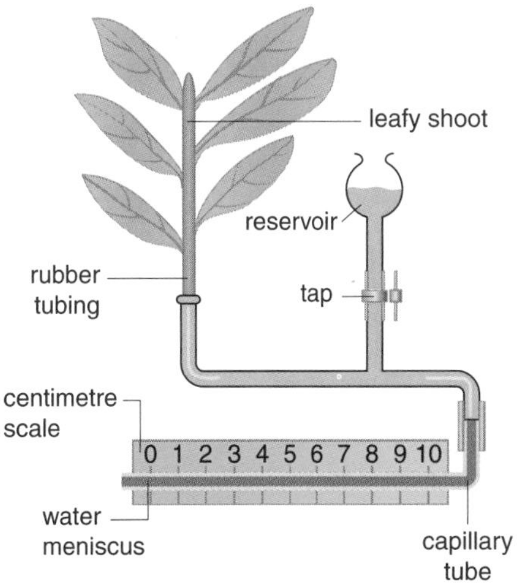

Ben measures the distance a bubble moves along the capillary tube to find out how much water has been lost. He finds that 9 mm³ was lost in 5 minutes. Calculate the rate of water loss from the plant in mm³/s. Show your workings.

_____

Rate of water loss = _____ mm³/s

leafy shoot
reservoir
rubber tubing
tap
centimetre scale
0 1 2 3 4 5 6 7 8 9 10
water meniscus
capillary tube

[2 marks]

4. Rebecca compares the transpiration rates of a plant with broad flat leaves and a plant with needles. She weighs the mass of the plants at the beginning of the experiment and then 24 hours later.

a Each plant has the same number of leaves. The plants are not watered during the 24 hours.

Give **two** other experimental conditions she should keep the same.

_____ [2 marks]

The table shows Rebecca's results.

	Plant A (broad, flat leaves)	Plant B (needles)
Mass at beginning (g)	252	137
Mass after 24 hours (g)	239	129

b Write a conclusion and explanation of Rebecca's results.

Use data/calculations in your answer.

_____

_____

_____ [3 marks]

Translocation

....

1. Describe what is meant by 'translocation'.

_____ [1 mark]

2. What happens to the dissolved sugars that are transported around a plant? Tick **one** box.

☐ They all get used in respiration.

☐ Some is stored and some is used for respiration.

☐ It is all used for photosynthesis to make oxygen.

☐ They are all used to make fruit. [1 mark]

3. How are root hair cells adapted for the efficient uptake of water?

_____ [1 mark]

4. Compare the structure and function of xylem and phloem.

_____

_____

_____

_____

_____

_____ [6 marks]

Microorganisms and disease

1. Give **one** example of each type of disease listed below.

   Non-communicable: _____

   Communicable: _____ [2 marks]

2. Draw **one** line from each pathogen to the disease it causes.

Viruses	Malaria
Bacteria	Flu
Protists	Athlete's foot
Fungi	Food poisoning

   [4 marks]

3. Cervical cancer occurs in the neck of the uterus.

   Scientists investigated the link between cervical cancer and infection with some types of Human Papilloma Virus (HPV).

   The graph shows the frequency of five different types of HPV in women who had cervical cancer.

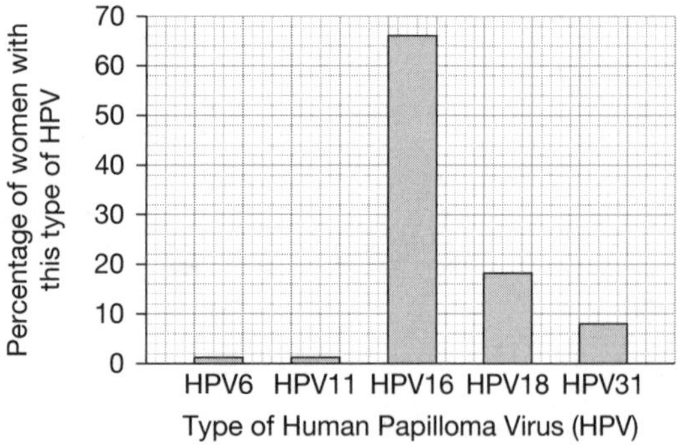

   A newspaper published an article about cervical cancer with the headline 'HPV causes cervical cancer'.

   Do the data shown in the graph support this claim? Explain your answer.

   _____

   _____

   _____

   _____ [4 marks]

Viral diseases

1. Viral diseases **cannot** be treated by antibiotics. Why? Tick **one** box.

☐ Viruses change their shape.   ☐ Viruses are not living things.

☐ Viruses live inside cells.   ☐ Viruses are too small.   [1 mark]

2. Measles is caused by a virus. A doctor vaccinates a child against measles.
What does the doctor inject to make the child immune to measles?

_____ [1 mark]

3. The swine flu virus is carried by pigs. The bird flu virus can spread much more quickly than the
swine flu virus. Suggest **two** reasons why.

_____

_____ [2 marks]

Bacterial diseases

1. Which statement about bacteria is correct? Tick **one** box.

☐ All bacteria are harmful.

☐ Bacteria can infect plants and animals.

☐ Bacterial diseases are caused by poor diet.

☐ All bacteria have the same size and shape.   [1 mark]

2. Students investigated the effect of five different antibiotics, A, B, C, D and E, on one type of bacterium. The diagram shows the Petri dish after three days.

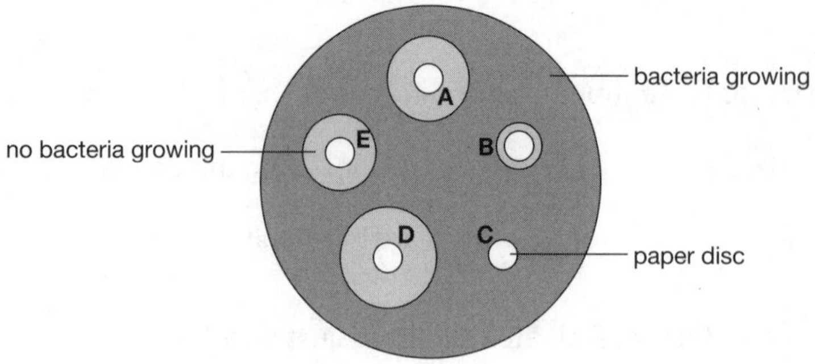

a Which antibiotic, A, B, C, D or E, would be **best** to treat a disease caused by this type of bacterium?

_____ [1 mark]

b Give the reason for your answer to part **a**.

_____ [1 mark]

> **Remember**
> The larger the clear zone around a disc in a Petri dish, the more bacteria have been killed. This shows that the chemical on that disc is more effective.

3. What are the symptoms of gonorrhoea? Tick **two** boxes.

☐ Headache ☐ Pain when urinating

☐ Rash ☐ Vomiting ☐ Yellow discharge [2 marks]

4. Name **two** ways that the spread of gonorrhoea can be controlled.

1. _____

2. _____ [2 marks]

Malaria

1. Malaria is caused by which type of pathogen? Tick **one** box.

☐ Bacteria ☐ Viruses ☐ Fungi ☐ Protists [1 mark]

2. The diagram shows stages in transmission of the malaria parasite by mosquitoes to humans.

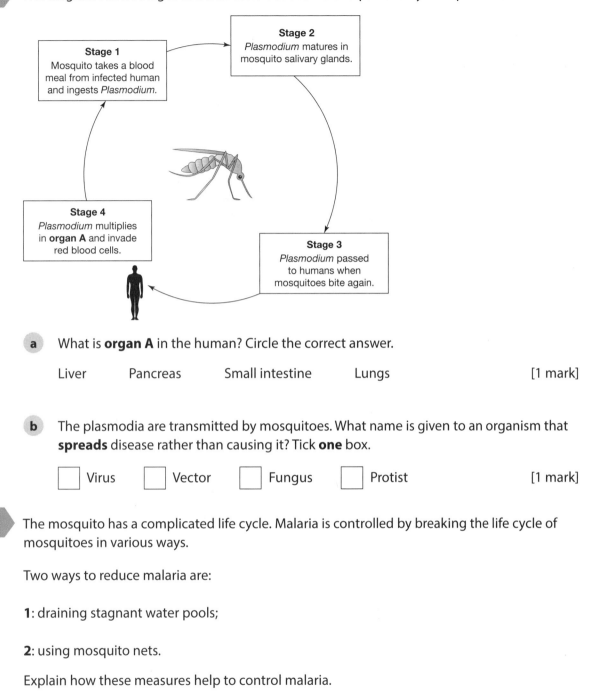

Stage 1
Mosquito takes a blood meal from infected human and ingests *Plasmodium.*

Stage 2
Plasmodium matures in mosquito salivary glands.

Stage 4
Plasmodium multiplies in **organ A** and invade red blood cells.

Stage 3
Plasmodium passed to humans when mosquitoes bite again.

a What is **organ A** in the human? Circle the correct answer.

Liver   Pancreas   Small intestine   Lungs   [1 mark]

b The plasmodia are transmitted by mosquitoes. What name is given to an organism that **spreads** disease rather than causing it? Tick **one** box.

☐ Virus   ☐ Vector   ☐ Fungus   ☐ Protist   [1 mark]

3. The mosquito has a complicated life cycle. Malaria is controlled by breaking the life cycle of mosquitoes in various ways.

Two ways to reduce malaria are:

1: draining stagnant water pools;

2: using mosquito nets.

Explain how these measures help to control malaria.

_____

_____

_____

_____ [4 marks]

Human defence systems

1. Draw **one** line from each part of the human defence system to its function.

White blood cells		Kills the majority of pathogens that enter via the mouth.
Stomach acid		Form scabs which seal the wound.
Platelets		Traps pathogens.
		Produce antimicrobial substances.

[3 marks]

2. The human body has several defences against viruses. Some prevent viruses from entering the body. Others act once the viruses have entered.

The diagram shows a white blood cell attacking a group of viruses. Complete it by drawing the second stage.

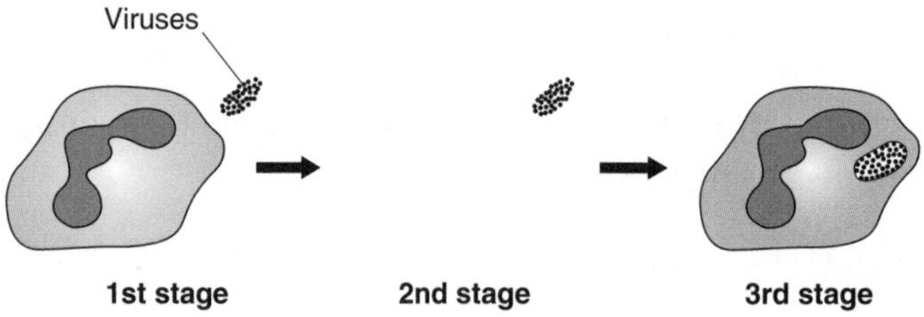

Viruses

1st stage   2nd stage   3rd stage

[2 marks]

3. Explain the adaptations of the respiratory system to protect against pathogens.

_____

_____

_____

_____ [4 marks]

Vaccination

1. In the sentences below, circle the correct underlined words or phrases to complete the sentences.

It is difficult to kill viruses inside the body because the virus: is not affected by drugs / lives inside cells / produces antitoxins. The vaccine contains an active / infective / inactive form of the virus. The vaccine stimulates the white blood cells to produce antibodies / antibiotics / drugs, which destroy the virus. [3 marks]

2. In the 1990s, many people thought that the measles, mumps and rubella (MMR) vaccine caused autism in some children. This is why the Japanese government stopped using the MMR vaccine.

The graph gives information about the percentage of Japanese children who developed autism during the 1990s.

> **Remember**
>
> With complex graphs like the one in Q2, it is easier to read the graph using the key. The bars show the percentage of children vaccinated. The line shows the number of children developing autism. This information is not clear from the axis labels alone.

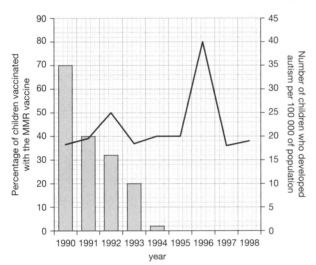

Key
▯ Percentage of children vaccinated with the MMR vaccine
— Number of children who developed autism per 100 000 of population

Maths **a** How many children developed autism per 100 000 of population in 1992?

_____ [1 mark]

b What is the percentage of children vaccinated with the MMR vaccine in 1996?

_____ [1 mark]

c   Is there a link between MMR vaccination and autism? Explain your answer.

_____

_____   [2 marks]

3.   Explain why new flu vaccines are made each year.

_____

_____

_____

_____   [4 marks]

Antibiotics and painkillers

. . . .

1.   Medicines contain useful drugs that relieve the symptoms caused by pathogens or kill the pathogens. Draw **one** line from each medicine to its correct function.

| Kill viruses without damaging human cells. |

| Antibiotics |

| Relieve symptoms of infection. |

| Painkillers |

| Kill bacteria by interfering with the process that makes bacterial cell walls. | [2 marks]

2.   Read the passage about the use of antibiotics in food production.

> People do not always agree about the use of antibiotics in food production.
>
> Some farmers put low doses of antibiotics in feed for cattle and sheep. Antibiotics help to keep the animals disease-free. Antibiotics also help the animals to grow.
>
> The use of antibiotics in livestock feed raises the risk of antibiotic-resistant bacteria developing. These could be dangerous to human health.

Worked Example   **a**   A student was asked to explain how a population of antibiotic-resistant bacteria might develop from non-resistant bacteria. Their answer is given below.   [3 marks]

42

Antibiotic will only kill non-resistant bacteria. If some bacteria survive, they will produce offspring thus increasing the population of resistant bacteria.

This response is only worthy of 2 marks. The student has an idea that some bacteria can survive the antibiotic – this gains 1 mark. The student also knows that the resistant bacteria breed and produce more resistant bacteria. However, the student should also have written about how the non-resistant bacteria become resistant – through mutation or variation.

Synoptic **b** Suggest **two** reasons why it is an advantage to keep farm animals disease-free.

_____

_____ [2 marks]

3. Why will antibiotics **not** get rid of flu?

_____

_____ [2 marks]

Remember
Q3 requires you to apply your knowledge that 1) antibiotics affect only bacteria and 2) flu is caused by a virus.

4. Explain the limitations of antibiotics.

_____

_____

_____ [3 marks]

Making and testing new drugs

1. Why must medical drugs be tested before they are used on patients?

Tick **all** boxes that apply.

☐ To check they work efficiently.

☐ To check they are safe to use.

☐ To make them as cheap as possible.

☐ To find the right dose.

☐ To check if they will work on animals.

Common misconception
On questions that ask you to 'tick all those that apply', do **not** assume that the marks awarded show how many ticks are needed. In this case, there are three ticks required but only **2** marks awarded.

[2 marks]

2. During clinical trials, new drugs are tested on animals and humans.

What would the new drug have been tested on before animals and humans?

_____ [1 mark]

3. Researchers sometimes use traditional medicines when starting to develop new drugs.

Draw **one** line from each medicine to match it with its correct source.

Heart drug digitalis	Willow trees
Painkiller aspirin	Foxgloves
Antibiotic penicillin	Tree bark
Anti-malarial quinine	Mould

[2 marks]

Monoclonal antibodies

1.

Synoptic

Higher Tier only

Monoclonal antibodies are produced by combining lymphocytes with a particular type of tumour cell. Which type of tumour cell is this? Tick **one** box.

Remember
Myeloma is a particular kind of tumour and is different from a carcinoma.

☐ Hybridoma   ☐ Lymphocyte

☐ Myeloma   ☐ Carcinoma

[1 mark]

2.

Higher Tier only

Which cells are produced when lymphocytes and myeloma cells combine? Tick **one** box.

☐ Antibodies   ☐ Hybridomas

☐ Memory lymphocytes   ☐ Platelets

[1 mark]

3.

Higher Tier only

Monoclonal antibodies are used for pregnancy testing.

Give **one** other use of monoclonal antibodies.

_____ [1 mark]

4. Read the statements about using monoclonal antibodies in humans. For each statement, tick whether it is true or false.

Higher Tier only

Statement	True	False
An advantage of using monoclonal antibodies is that healthy body cells are not affected.		
Monoclonal antibodies create more side effects than expected.		
Monoclonal antibodies are produced in humans.		
Monoclonal antibodies cannot be used to treat cancer.		

[4 marks]

5. The diagram shows the parts of a pregnancy test strip.

Higher Tier only

Worked Example

The strip will show a positive test result when a woman is pregnant. A student was asked to explain how the pregnancy test strip works to show a positive result. [3 marks]

4. Control window: Immobilised antibodies specific to the mobile antibodies from the reaction zone.

3. Result window: Immobilised antibodies specific to hCG.

2. Reaction zone: There are mobile antibodies specific to hCG here. These antibodies can move and have blue dye attached to them.

1. Urine applied here.

Pregnancy tests are designed to tell if your urine contains a hormone called human chorionic gonadotropin (hCG). This hormone is produced right after an egg gets fertilised. When a woman's urine comes in contact with the specially treated strip on a pregnancy test stick, results appear within minutes, indicating whether or not hCG is present. The results show up in two windows.

This response did not receive any credit as it was far too general – although factually correct in some places. The question requires an understanding of how monoclonal antibodies work. Use the diagram to help you structure the response. If urine is applied to one end, then it must mean that it travels along the stick. There are hCG antibodies in the reaction zone. What will happen if there are hCG molecules in the urine? The hCG molecules in the reaction zone are attached to blue dye to make them visible. When they get to the result window, any hCG molecules will attach to immobilised antibodies and since they also have the dye attached, there will be a line visible in the result window. The result will be further confirmed when the unattached hCG molecules travel to the control window, where they will attach to the immobilised antibodies there.

Plant fungal diseases

1. Plants can suffer from a disease called black spot. This causes black or purple spots on the upper surface of leaves. What causes black spot in plants? Tick **one** box.

☐ Aphids   ☐ Viruses   ☐ Fungi   ☐ Mineral deficiency   [1 mark]

2. A gardener notices spots on the leaves of her rose plants. She is not sure what type of plant disease is causing this. Suggest **two** methods to identify the disease.

Higher Tier only

1. _____

2. _____ [2 marks]

3. In recent years, rose black spot has become more common in urban gardens.

Untreated, black spot can quickly affect all the roses in a garden.

Higher Tier only   **a**   Explain how the pathogen affects growth.

_____

_____

_____ [3 marks]

b   Describe how the fungus is transmitted.

_____

_____

_____

_____ [4 marks]

c A student is asked to explain four treatments for rose black spot. [4 marks]

Since the disease is caused by fungus that produces spores, it is really important to make sure that the affected leaves and stems are removed immediately and burned. If the infected plant is allowed to remain untreated, the spores can be spread by rain or wind. In addition, fungicides can help kill the fungus.

This answer is worth 3 marks because the student has described three main points about immediate removal of stems and leaves and the need to burn them. The student also mentions fungicides. A further mark can be gained by showing an understanding that infected parts of the plant should not be composted as spores can survive and re-infect other rose plants.

4. To detect and identify plant diseases accurately, testing kits using monoclonal antibodies can be used. However, plants do **not** produce antibodies.

Higher Tier only Suggest how monoclonal antibody testing kits can be used to identify a plant disease.

_____

_____

_____ [2 marks]

Other plant diseases

1. Name **two** primary barriers that plants have to defend against attack from pathogens.

_____ and _____ [2 marks]

2. Tobacco mosaic virus is a disease affecting plants. Gardeners should wash **all** tools used on plants with tobacco mosaic virus with disinfectant. Suggest why.

_____ [1 mark]

3. Tobacco mosaic virus causes plants to produce less chlorophyll. This leads to leaf discolouration. Explain why plants with tobacco mosaic virus have stunted growth. [2 marks]

_____

_____

4. Plants need certain nutrients to grow well. The table shows two of these.

Nutrients	Part played in the plant
Nitrates	Making proteins – building blocks of all plant material
Magnesium	Making chlorophyll for photosynthesis

At a plant clinic, people turn up with plants that are **not** growing well. For each plant, explain what is wrong with it. Suggest what needs to be done to the soil to make sure that the plant grows well.

a Plant A has pale leaves with yellow patches and green veins. It is **not** growing well.

_____

_____

_____ [2 marks]

b Plant B shows **very stunted growth**, even though it gets lots of light and is well watered.

_____

_____

_____

_____ [2 marks]

Remember

Yellowing leaves with green veins indicate a magnesium deficiency. Yellowing leaves with stunted growth show that the plant is not getting enough nitrates.

Plant defence responses

1. Plants have physical defences that are barriers to prevent microbial pathogens entering. Draw **one** line from each adaptation to match it with its function.

Layers of dead cells around stems	To prevent pathogens entering cells.
Waxy leaf cuticle	To prevent pests from entering living cells underneath.
Cellulose cell walls	To prevent pathogens entering the epidermis.

[3 marks]

2. Plants have mechanical adaptations to help defend themselves.

The image shows a nettle plant.

Explain how the nettle is adapted for defence and protection.

_____

_____

_____

_____

[2 marks]

3. Plants use chemicals to defend themselves from attack by microorganisms.

Below are examples of ways that plants protect themselves. For each adaptation, draw a circle around the type of response described.

Adaptation   **Type of response**

Adaptation	Type of response
Leaves droop or curl when touched.	Physical / mechanical / chemical
Production of poisons that taste bad.	Physical / mechanical / chemical
Cellulose cell walls.	Physical / mechanical / chemical

[3 marks]

4. Female butterflies lay their eggs on leaves. The eggs hatch into caterpillars that eat leaves and other plant parts. This damages the plant.

Passion flower leaves have markings that look like butterfly eggs. This type of mechanical defence is called **mimicry**. Suggest why it helps protect the passion flower plant.

_____

_____

_____

[2 marks]

Photosynthesis reaction

1. Use the words from the box to complete the sentences.

| light | heat | leaves | stems | mitochondria | chemical | chloroplasts |

Photosynthesis is a chemical reaction which happens in the

_____ of green plants.

During photosynthesis _____
energy is absorbed by chlorophyll, a green substance found

in _____ in some plant and
algae cells. [3 marks]

Common misconception
Many people think plants get their food from the soil, but this is a misconception. A plant makes its own 'food' in the form of glucose by the process of photosynthesis. Plants have evolved to harvest energy from the Sun to produce their own supply of glucose.

2. Complete the word equation for photosynthesis.

_____ + water $\xrightarrow{\text{light}}$ glucose + _____ [2 marks]

3. Photosynthesis takes in energy from light during photosynthesis. What term **best** describes a reaction that takes in energy? Tick **one** box.

☐ Exothermic ☐ Endothermic ☐ Physical ☐ Chemical [1 mark]

4. Name the chemical reaction used by plants to obtain energy from glucose.

_____ [1 mark]

5. Why is photosynthesis the first step in 'making food for every animal on the planet'?

_____

_____

_____ [2 marks]

Rate of photosynthesis

1. List **three** factors that limit the rate of photosynthesis.

_____ [3 marks]

2. Elena investigates the rate of photosynthesis in *Cabomba* pondweed.

Required Practical

She has this apparatus:

- 7 cm-long pieces of pondweed
- beaker
- funnel
- lamp

- metre ruler
- stop clock
- 1% sodium hydrogen carbonate (or water)

a *Cabomba* produces bubbles of oxygen as it photosynthesises. Using this apparatus, describe a method Elena could use to investigate the effects of light intensity on the rate of photosynthesis in pondweed.

Your answer should include:

- what you would measure
- what variables you would control.

_____

_____

_____

_____

_____

_____ [6 marks]

Maths **b** Elena's results are shown in the table.

Distance from lamp [cm]	Number of bubbles produced in a minute			
	Test 1	Test 2	Test 3	Mean
10	46	39	42	
15	34	31	29	
20	21	23	24	

Complete the missing values in the table by calculating the mean number of bubbles produced for each distance from the lamp. Give your answers to 3 significant figures.

_____ [3 marks]

c Give **two** reasons why counting bubbles is **not** the most accurate way of measuring the amount of oxygen given off.

_____

_____ [2 marks]

d Write a conclusion about the effect of light intensity on the rate of photosynthesis. Use the information in the table.

_____ [1 mark]

3.

The inverse square law allows you to calculate how much light falls on pondweed at different distances from the light source. It is calculated using this formula:

$$\text{Light intensity} = \frac{1}{distance^2}$$

Distance from lamp (cm)	Light intensity (arbitrary units)
10	0.01
15	0.004
20	_____

Use the formula to calculate the light intensity for 20 cm. Write your answer in the table.

_____ [1 mark]

4.

Higher Tier only

Light intensity obeys the inverse square law. This means that if you double the distance you:

Tick **one** box.

☐ Quarter the intensity   ☐ Halve the intensity

☐ Double the intensity   ☐ Minus the intensity   [1 mark]

Limiting factors

1. Higher Tier only

1. A scientist monitors the concentration of dissolved oxygen in a pond over a 24-hour period. She finds that the dissolved oxygen concentration is always highest at about 4 pm. Explain her findings.

_____

_____ [2 marks]

2. Margery want to speed up the growth of her tomato plants. She puts them in a greenhouse with a paraffin heater. List **two** ways this could speed up the growth.

_____

_____ [2 marks]

3. The graph shows how carbon dioxide concentration affects the rate of photosynthesis.

Worked Example

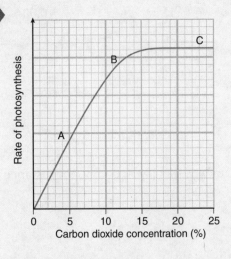

Remember

For the exam you will be expected to extract information and interpret graphs about rates of photosynthesis and limiting factors. Make sure you can explain 'rate of photosynthesis' graphs for carbon dioxide, light and temperature.

a Describe and explain the shape of the curve between points A, B and C. [4 marks]

A student's answer to this question is given here.

Between A and B the rate of photosynthesis increases linearly with increasing carbon dioxide concentration.

The student has used the term 'linear', which accurately describes the relationship.

Between B and C gradually the rate decreases, and at a certain carbon dioxide concentration the rate of photosynthesis becomes constant.

At point C a rise in carbon dioxide concentration has no effect on the rate of photosynthesis.

It is good practice to use actual figures from the graph in a description. It would be better to say 'at 15% carbon dioxide concentration'.

Although the student has written a description, they have not explained what they have described so they would only get 2 of the 4 marks. They would need to explain the description by saying that between A and B the rate of photosynthesis increases with carbon dioxide concentration, because carbon dioxide is needed for photosynthesis, so the more there is, the faster the rate. Between B and C, the rate does not increase because other factors such as light intensity become limiting.

b The concentration of carbon dioxide in the air is 0.04%. Use information in the graph to explain whether a gardener could make plants in his greenhouse grow faster by giving them extra carbon dioxide.

Higher Tier only

_____

_____ [2 mark]

Uses of glucose from photosynthesis

1. Use the words from the box to complete the sentences.

| starch | glycogen | storage | respiration | insulation | growth | energy |

The glucose produced by a plant during photosynthesis is converted into

_____, fats and oils for _____.

Some glucose is used to make cellulose for cell walls, and proteins for

_____ and repair. It is also used by the plant to

release energy by _____. [4 marks]

2. Which of the following statements are true? Tick **two** boxes.

☐ All plant cells carry out photosynthesis in the day and then switch to respiration at night.

☐ Plant cells can photosynthesise at day or night depending on when they need to produce glucose.

☐ Plant cells respire all the time, but some also carry out photosynthesis when light is available.

☐ Only some plant cells can carry out photosynthesis; some, such as root hair cells, do not. [2 marks]

> **Common misconception**
> Some students think all plant cells carry out photosynthesis in the day and respiration at night. However, plant cells actually respire all the time because their cells need energy to stay alive. Photosynthesis can only happen when there is light, which is why plants can only photosynthesise in the day or under artificial light.

3. The part of the potato plant we eat is the tuber. It is an enlarged underground stem that stores starch for the plant. New potato plants grow from potato tubers.

Suggest how new potato plants obtain energy needed for growth.

_____

_____ [1 mark]

4. Explain why the potato plant no longer needs this energy source once it has grown above the soil.

_____

_____ [1 mark]

5. Why do the tubers store starch, **not** glucose?

_____ [1 mark]

6. Explain why a plant that does **not** absorb enough nitrate ions might have stunted growth.

_____

_____

_____ [2 marks]

Cell respiration

1. Use the words from the box to complete the sentences.

| glucose | cells | aerobically | anaerobically | nuclei | mitochondria | oxygen |

Respiration is a series of reactions in which energy is released from the reactant, which is

_____. Respiration can take place _____

(uses oxygen) or _____ (without oxygen) in the form of respiration

that uses oxygen. Aerobic respiration happens inside the _____
found in cells. [4 marks]

2. Which of the following statements about respiration is true? Tick **one** box.

☐ Respiration is another name for breathing.

☐ Glucose is produced during respiration.

☐ Respiration does not happen when the body is at rest.

☐ Respiration releases energy from glucose. [1 mark]

3. Complete the word equation for aerobic respiration:

glucose + _____ ⟶ carbon dioxide + _____ (+ energy) [2 marks]

4. Give **two** ways an organism uses the energy released from respiration.

_____ [2 marks]

5. Explain why respiration is an exothermic reaction.

_____ [1 mark]

6. Some of the energy transferred by respiration in our cells is used to synthesise new molecules that the body needs. Give **two** examples of smaller molecules that are linked together to form larger molecules using energy from respiration.

_____

_____ [2 marks]

7. Long-distance runners often eat meals containing a lot of carbohydrate over three days before a race. How does this help muscles to work well during a race? [2 marks]

Worked Example

A student's answer to this question is given here.

The carbohydrate provides the glucose needed for respiration.

This is correct and would gain 1 mark. But to get 2 marks, you would need to say that the runner's muscle cells will use lots of energy to contract during the race, so a good supply of glucose will enable the muscles to respire at a faster rate.

Anaerobic respiration

1. What does the word **anaerobic** mean? Tick **one** box. [1 mark]

☐ With oxygen   ☐ Without oxygen   ☐ No energy   ☐ Without carbon dioxide

2. What is the product of anaerobic respiration in muscle cells?

_____ [1 mark]

3. Explain why our cells normally respire aerobically, rather than anaerobically.

_____

_____ [2 marks]

4. Oliver is sprinting away from a bull. Explain what type of respiration takes place in his muscle cells when he begins to sprint. What type of respiration occurs after sprinting for several minutes?

_____

_____

_____ [3 marks]

5. Complete the word equation to show anaerobic respiration in plant and yeast cells.

glucose $\longrightarrow$ _____ + _____ [2 marks]

6. Anaerobic respiration in yeast cells is called fermentation.

Give **two** uses of fermentation.

_____ [2 marks]

7. Compare anaerobic respiration in a yeast cell with anaerobic respiration in a muscle cell.

_____

_____

_____ [3 marks]

Command words

The command word 'compare' requires a description of the similarities and/or differences between things. Make sure you do not just write about one.

Response to exercise

1. Use the words in the box to complete the sentences.

| deoxygenated | breathing volume | oxygenated | glucose |
| carbon dioxide | carbon monoxide | energy | |

When you exercise, your heart rate, breathing rate and _____

increase to supply the muscles with more _____ blood.

The blood delivers oxygen and _____ to the respiring muscle

cells and takes away _____ . [4 marks]

2. Which statement **best** describes what happens when muscles become fatigued during vigorous activity? Tick **one** box.

☐ They work more efficiently. ☐ They work less efficiently.

☐ They stop contracting. ☐ They produce urea. [1 mark]

3. Explain why a person continues to breathe heavily after strenuous exercise has stopped.

_____

_____ [2 marks]

4. The graph shows how oxygen uptake by the lungs changes during exercise and recovery.

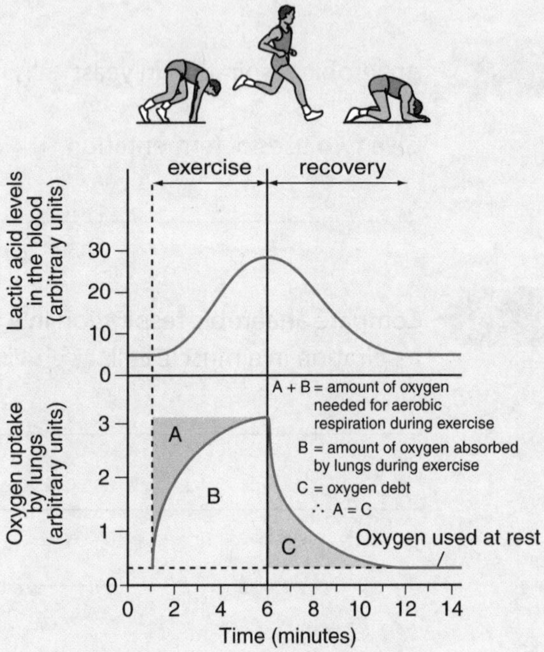

Which area shows:

a The amount of oxygen absorbed by the lungs during exercise?

_____ [1 mark]

b The amount of oxygen needed for aerobic respiration during exercise?

_____ [1 mark]

c The oxygen debt?

_____ [1 mark]

d Explain why areas A and C are the same size.

_____ [1 mark]

60

Homeostasis

. . . .

1. Which things from the list below need to be controlled by homeostasis?

Tick **two** boxes.

☐ Carbon dioxide ☐ Red blood cells ☐ Water

☐ Skin colour ☐ Respiration [2 marks]

2. What part of the body monitors water, temperature and carbon dioxide levels in the blood?

_____ [1 mark]

3. What is the optimum temperature for the body's enzymes?

Tick **one** box.

☐ 0°C ☐ 100°C ☐ 54°C ☐ 28°C ☐ 37°C [1 mark]

4. Read the statements and circle the **correct** response.

Hormones travel around the body in the form of electrical impulses. TRUE / FALSE

Organs that secrete hormones are called glands. TRUE / FALSE

Hormones are carried all over the body but only affect target organs. TRUE / FALSE

There are three control systems responsible for homeostasis. TRUE / FALSE

Effectors that bring about a response can be muscles or glands. TRUE / FALSE

[5 marks]

5. There are **three** organs of the body involved in excretion – what are they and what do they excrete?

Complete the table below.

Organ	Substance excreted

[3 marks]

The nervous system and reflexes

1. A student accidentally touches a sharp object. Her hand immediately pulls away.

The diagram shows the structures involved in this response.

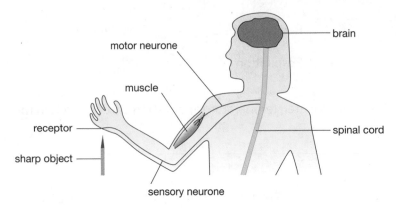

Use the correct word or phrase from the diagram to complete each sentence.

The stimulus is detected by the _____. Impulses travel

to the central nervous system along a cell called a _____.

Impulses travel from the central nervous system to the effector along a cell called

a _____. The hand is pulled away from the sharp

object by the _____. [4 marks]

2. The nerve pathway in the reflex action shown by the diagram
is 1.5 metres in length. A nerve impulse travels at 75 metres
per second.

> **Maths**
> To find the time taken,
> divide the length by the
> speed of the nerve impulse.
> The unit for speed is metres
> per second; therefore, the
> unit for time is seconds.

a Use this information to calculate the time taken for this
reflex action.

Show your working out clearly.

_____

Time taken for reflex action = _____ seconds [1 mark]

b The actual interval is longer than the interval calculated in part **a** .

Explain the difference.

_____ [1 mark]

3. Two students investigate reflex action times.

Required practical

1. Student **A** sits with her elbow resting on the edge of a table.

2. Student **B** holds a ruler with the bottom of the ruler level with A's thumb.

3. Student **B** drops the ruler.

4. Student **A** catches the ruler and records the distance.

5. Steps **1** to **4** are then repeated.

Student B

Student A

Suggest **two** ways the students could improve the method to make sure the test would give valid results.

_____

_____

_____ [2 marks]

4. In an experiment, students measured reaction time using a computer program.

Required practical

This is the method used.

1. The computer shows a red box at the start.

2. As soon as the box turns green the student presses a key on the keyboard as fast as possible.

3. The test is repeated five times and a mean reaction time is displayed.

Using a computer program to measure reaction times is likely to be more valid than the method using a dropped ruler.

Give **two** reasons why.

_____

_____ [2 marks]

The brain

....

1. Which are the **main parts** of the brain?

Tick **three** boxes.

☐	Cornea	☐	Cerebellum
☐	Cerebral palsy	☐	Meninges
☐	Medulla	☐	Cerebral cortex [2 marks]

> **Remember**
> You need to select three answers for 2 marks. The marks are usually distributed so that three correct answers are awarded 2 marks, while two correct answers are awarded 1 mark. One correct answer does not gain any credit.

2. Match the functions below to the parts you have chosen in Q1. Write the correct part of the brain in the table below.

Function	Part of brain
Controls unconscious activity such as heartbeat and breathing.	_____
Responsible for higher order functions such as language and memory.	_____
Coordinates muscle activity.	_____

[3 marks]

3. Some people have a condition in which information from the skin does **not** reach the brain.

Explain why this is dangerous for the person.

_____

_____

_____ [2 marks]

4. A man has a head injury. He staggers and sways as he walks.

Suggest which part of his brain has been damaged.

_____ [1 mark]

The eye

• •

1. When a bright light shines in the eye, a number of changes occur.

Which of the following statements is **incorrect**? Tick **one** box.

☐ Impulses travel in the optic nerve.

☐ The radial fibres in the iris contract.

☐ The retina responds.

☐ The pupil becomes smaller.   [1 mark]

2. The diagram shows the structure of the human eye.

Label the diagram with the parts in the box below.

optic nerve   ciliary muscle   retina
cornea   suspensory ligaments

[5 marks]

3. Receptor cells in the eye convert light into nerve impulses.
There are **two** main types of receptor cells. Name them.

_____   [1 marks]

4. What is the purpose of rod cells in the eye?

_____   [1 mark]

5. Describe fully the path a ray of light will take through the eye.

_____

_____

_____

_____

_____

_____

_____   [5 marks]

Command words

The command word **describe** means to give a full account of the structures in the eye that a ray of light will travel through. Don't stop at the retina, but carry on to describe how light will be converted to chemical signals to travel to the brain.

Seeing in focus

1. Structures in the human eye help bend light onto receptor cells to produce a sharp focus.

Select the correct statement about these structures. Tick **one** box.

☐ The lens is responsible for bending most of the light rays entering the eye.

☐ The shape of the cornea can change.

☐ The shape of the lens can change.

☐ Receptor cells are found in the optic nerve.

☐ The suspensory ligaments holding the lens can contract and relax. [1 mark]

2. Some people wear glasses to improve their vision.

Figure 1 shows light entering the eye in a person with blurred vision.

Figure 2 shows how this condition is corrected with glasses.

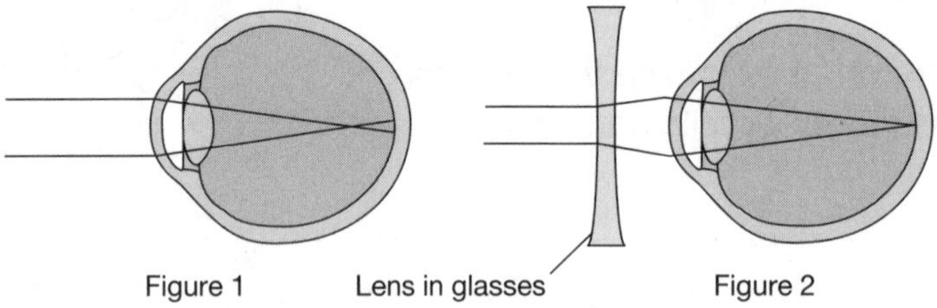

Figure 1   Lens in glasses   Figure 2

a What type of eye defect does the person have?

_____ [1 mark]

b Explain how the blurred vision is corrected.

_____

_____ [2 marks]

3. Some new technologies are available to correct eye defects.

Name **two** of these technologies.

_____ [2 marks]

4. Describe the changes taking place in the eye when:

a focusing on a near object;

_____

_____

_____

_____ [3 marks]

b focusing on a distant object.

_____

_____

_____

_____ [3 marks]

5. A student was asked to explain what myopia is and how it can be corrected. [4 marks]

Worked Example

Myopia is when people can't see far away objects and need to use glasses or contact lenses to see properly. It happens when the lens can't stretch and light cannot reach the retina.

This answer is only credited with 1 mark for recognising that myopia is short-sightedness. The student needed to say the type of lens needed in glasses to correct myopia (concave). The explanation of why myopia occurs is incorrect.

Control of body temperature

. . . .

1. Choose the **two** most appropriate words or phrases from the box to complete the sentence.

| touch and pressure | ultraviolet light | bacteria | evaporation of water |
| heat from the Sun | body temperature |

The skin helps to control _____ and

_____.   [2 marks]

2. A student swallowed some iced water. The graph shows how this affected his skin temperature and brain temperature.

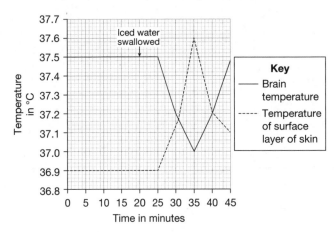

a Explain why the brain temperature changed **after** swallowing the iced water.

_____

_____   [2 marks]

b This change in brain temperature led to a change in the temperature of the surface layer of the skin.

Explain how this happened.

_____

_____

_____   [3 marks]

3.

The temperature at the surface of the skin can be measured by using thermography. Areas with higher temperature appear as a different colour on the thermographs.

The drawings show thermographs before and after exercise.

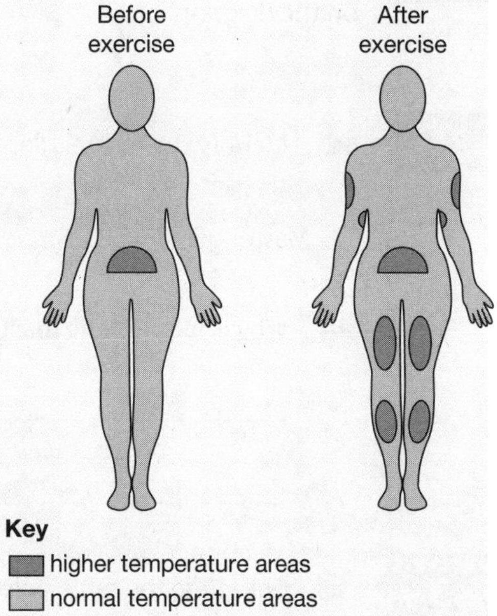

Explain the body mechanisms which affect skin temperature to give the results shown in the drawing.

Before exercise   After exercise

Key

higher temperature areas

normal temperature areas

_____

_____

_____

_____

_____

_____   [6 marks]

Hormones and the endocrine system

1.

Information is passed to target organs in the body by hormones.

a How do hormones travel around the body?

_____   [1 mark]

b What name is given to the organs that secrete hormones?

_____   [1 mark]

2. Write the names of glands **A** and **B** on the diagram.

[2 marks]

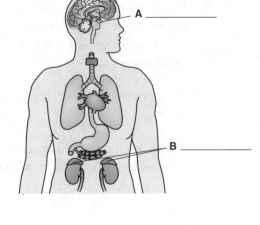

A _____

B _____

3. **a** Identify the master gland from **2** above.

Master gland = _____ [1 mark]

b Why is it called the master gland?

_____

_____ [1 mark]

4. **a** Complete the table below to show which hormone is secreted by which gland.

Gland / organ	Hormone
_____	Follicle stimulating hormone (FSH)
Thyroid	_____
_____	Adrenaline
Ovaries	_____

[4 marks]

b The pituitary gland produces hormones that have a direct effect on their target organs. Some pituitary hormones have an indirect effect – they cause other glands to secrete hormones.

Describe **two** hormones produced by the pituitary and their effects on their organs.

[6 marks]

A student's answer to this question is given below.

The pituitary gland produces thyroid-stimulating hormone which acts on the thyroid gland. It also produces the hormone FSH that makes the ovaries release oestrogen.

This answer gains 5 marks out of a possible 6; 2 marks for correctly stating the hormone the pituitary gland produces and the target organ for that hormone. However, 1 mark was lost because there is no mention of what the target organ does after it is stimulated by the hormone. The second sentence gains full credit as the student has stated correctly the name of the hormone, the target organ and the response.

Controlling blood glucose

1. The graph shows the changes in the blood glucose level of two boys, Patrick and Glen.

Both boys had no food intake for 12 hours before taking an energy drink at time 0.

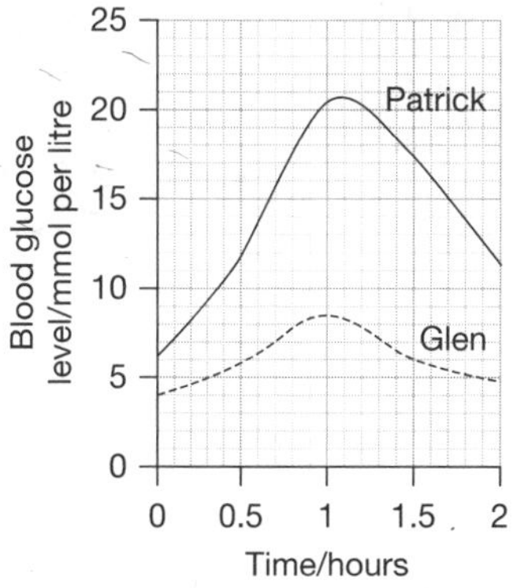

a Use evidence from the graph to identify which of these boys has diabetes.

_____ [1 mark]

b State another symptom of diabetes that this boy might have.

_____ [1 mark]

c Why do people with Type 1 diabetes need to take insulin?

_____

_____ [2 marks]

2. Explain what happens if **too much** insulin is taken.

_____

_____ [2 marks]

3. How does the body of a healthy person restore blood sugar levels if the level drops too low?

Higher Tier only

_____

_____

_____ [3 marks]

Maintaining water balance in the body

1. The table shows the mean daily input (water gain) and output (water loss) of water for an adult.

Water gain		Water loss	
Source	Volume (dm³)	Route	Volume (dm³)
Food	1.0	Urine	_____
Drink	1.5	Faeces	0.1
Respiration	0.4	Lungs	0.4
		Skin	0.9
Total	2.9	Total	2.9

a Calculate the mean daily output of urine. Write it in the table.

_____ [1 mark]

b Approximately what proportion of water gained by the body comes from food?

Tick **one** box.

☐ 1/4   ☐ 1/3   ☐ 1/2   ☐ 1/8   [1 mark]

c On a hotter day, the volumes of water lost and gained will be different.

What differences will there be? Tick **two** boxes.

☐ More sweat produced.   ☐ More faeces produced.

☐ More food eaten.   ☐ Less urine produced.

☐ Less liquid drunk.   [2 marks]

2. Some molecules need to be absorbed back into the blood rather than excreted in urine. This is called **selective reabsorption**.

Which of the following substances is **not** selectively reabsorbed? Tick **one** box.

☐ Water   ☐ Glucose   ☐ Chloride ions

☐ Urea   ☐ Sodium ions

[1 mark]

Water and nitrogen balance in the body

1.

Higher Tier only

Proteins are digested to smaller molecules.

Which of the following substances is a product of protein digestion? Tick **one** box.

☐ Lipids   ☐ Glucose   ☐ Ammonia   ☐ Urea   ☐ Amino acids   [1 mark]

2.

Higher Tier only

ADH effects the permeability of the kidney tubules.

Which of the following glands produces ADH? Tick **one** box.

☐ Adrenal   ☐ Pituitary   ☐ Thyroid   ☐ Hypothalamus

[1 mark]

3.

Higher Tier only

Describe how excess amino acids are processed by the liver before being excreted by the kidney.

_____

_____

_____

_____ [4 marks]

4.

Higher Tier only

Explain how ADH controls the amount of water excreted by the kidneys.

_____

_____

_____

_____

_____

_____ [6 marks]

Hormones in human reproduction

1. Complete the table below.

Hormone	Organ where it is produced	Function of hormone
Oestrogen	_____	Female reproductive hormone
_____	Testes	Male reproductive hormone

[2 marks]

2. Hormones regulate the functions of many organs. Complete the following sentences.

Hormones control the monthly release of an egg from the woman's _____.

Hormones also control the thickness of the lining of her _____. Hormones given

to women to stimulate the release of eggs are called _____ drugs. [3 marks]

3. Describe the roles of FSH and LH in the menstrual cycle.

_____

_____

_____ [2 marks]

Hormones interacting in human reproduction

1.

Higher Tier only

In humans, fertilisation can only occur within a few days of a woman ovulating.

The graphs show hormone levels during the menstrual cycle.

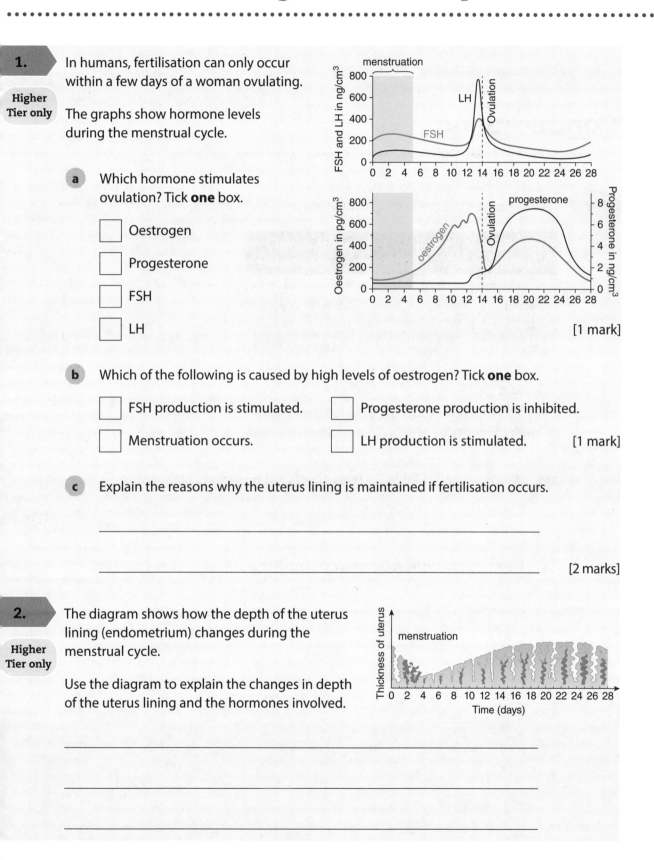

a Which hormone stimulates ovulation? Tick **one** box.

- [ ] Oestrogen
- [ ] Progesterone
- [ ] FSH
- [ ] LH

[1 mark]

b Which of the following is caused by high levels of oestrogen? Tick **one** box.

- [ ] FSH production is stimulated.
- [ ] Progesterone production is inhibited.
- [ ] Menstruation occurs.
- [ ] LH production is stimulated.

[1 mark]

c Explain the reasons why the uterus lining is maintained if fertilisation occurs.

_____

_____ [2 marks]

2.

Higher Tier only

The diagram shows how the depth of the uterus lining (endometrium) changes during the menstrual cycle.

Use the diagram to explain the changes in depth of the uterus lining and the hormones involved.

_____

_____

_____

_____

_____

_____

[6 marks]

Contraception

....

1. Table 1 shows some methods of contraception.

Type of contraception	Percentage (%) of pregnancies prevented
Oral pill	>99
Implant	99
Condom	98
Diaphragm	<96

a Which method in Table 1 is **least** effective at preventing pregnancy?

_____ [1 mark]

b Which method will protect against sexually transmitted diseases like HIV?

_____ [1 mark]

Another method of contraception is the intrauterine device (IUD).

There are two main types of IUD: copper, and plastic.

Both types of IUD are more than 99% effective. Look at Table 2:

	Copper IUD	Plastic IUD
How the IUD works	• releases copper • copper changes the fluids in the uterus to kill sperm	• releases a hormone • hormone thickens mucus from the cervix so the sperm have more difficulty swimming to the egg
Benefits	• prevents pregnancy for up to 10 years • can be removed at any time • can be used as emergency contraception	• prevents pregnancy for up to 5 years • can be removed at any time
Possible side effects	• very painful periods • heavy periods or periods which last for a long time • feeling sick, back pain	• painful periods • light periods or no periods • hormones may affect mood • ovarian cysts

c Evaluate the use of the plastic IUD as a contraceptive compared to the copper IUD.

Use the information in Table 2.

_____

_____

_____

_____

_____

_____ [4 marks]

Command words

The command word 'evaluate' means to judge from available evidence. An evaluation goes further than a 'compare question'. You will need to write down some of the points for and against both types of IUD to develop an argument.

2. Below are some facts about using birth control pills.

Which facts show the advantages of using birth control pills? Tick **three** boxes.

☐ Birth control pills are 99% effective in preventing pregnancy.

☐ The hormones in the pills have some rare but serious side effects.

☐ This method of birth control gives no protection against sexually transmitted diseases.

☐ The hormones in the pills give protection against some women's diseases.

☐ The woman has to remember to take the pill every day.

☐ The woman's monthly periods become more regular.   [3 marks]

Using hormones to treat infertility

1. For women who are **unable** to conceive, hormones can be given as a fertility drug.

Higher Tier only

Which hormones can be used to treat infertility? Tick **two** boxes.

☐ Adrenaline   ☐ Thyroxine   ☐ FSH

☐ Oestrogen   ☐ LH   ☐ Testosterone   [2 marks]

2. These are some advantages and disadvantages of using fertility and contraceptive drugs.

Higher Tier only

What are the **disadvantages** of using fertility and contraceptive drugs? Tick **three** boxes.

☐ Prevent unwanted pregnancy.

☐ May increase chance of getting a sexually transmitted disease.

☐ May cause side-effects in female body.

☐ Regulate the menstrual cycle.

☐ Prolonged use may prevent later ovulation.

☐ Can stimulate egg release.

☐ May cause multiple births.   [3 marks]

3.

Higher Tier only

Read the passage about fertility treatment.

> During normal IVF, a woman undergoes several weeks of hormone injections.
>
> This treatment can lead to a condition called ovarian hyperstimulation syndrome resulting in a build-up of fluid in the lungs. Very rarely, it can cause death. The syndrome occurs in about 1% of standard IVF cycles, but in about 10% of the IVF cycles of some women. An IVF cycle may cost up to £4300.
>
> In IVM, hormone treatment lasts for less than 7 days. Eggs are collected from the ovaries while they are still immature. Each egg is then matured in a laboratory for up to 48 hours before being injected with a single sperm.
>
> A few days after fertilisation, the embryos are implanted into the mother's womb. The cost of each IVM cycle is £1700.
>
> An IVM expert says: 'In IVM treatment there's a small risk of abnormalities in the sex chromosomes and also of birth deformities and cancer in the babies. These risks are not massive but they are greater than in IVF.'

Evaluate the use of IVM rather than IVF in treating infertility.

Remember to give a conclusion to your evaluation.

_____

_____

_____

_____ [4 marks]

Negative feedback

1.

Higher Tier only

Human body temperature is 37°C. When a person is in a hot environment where the air temperature is much higher than 37°C, changes take place to make sure their body temperature remains at 37°C.

   a Explain **two** changes that take place in the body to keep its temperature at 37°C in a hot environment.

_____

_____ [2 marks]

b   Homeostasis involves negative feedback.

With reference to body temperature, describe what is meant by the term 'negative feedback'.

_____

_____

_____   [3 marks]

2.   Blood glucose concentration is an example of a negative feedback mechanism.

Higher Tier only

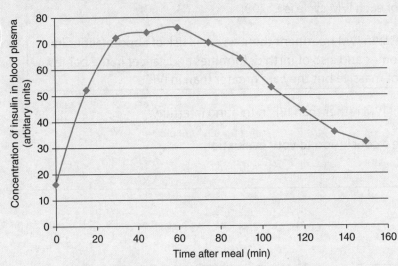

Time after meal (min)

Use the graph to explain why blood glucose concentration is an example of negative feedback.

_____

_____

_____

_____   [4 marks]

Plant hormones

1.

Required practical

A student investigated growth in plants.

The student:

- planted a seed in damp soil in a plant pot

- put the plant pot in a dark cupboard.

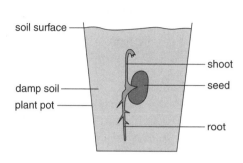

The diagram shows the result after 5 days.

Draw a circle around the correct underlined answer to complete each sentence.

a After the 5 days, the root had grown <u>away from water / in the direction of the force of gravity / towards light</u>. [1 mark]

b After the 5 days, the shoot had grown <u>towards water / away from light / against the force of gravity</u>. [1 mark]

c After the plant had grown, the student put the plant pot by a window with lots of light (diagram on the left). Complete the diagram on the right to show the appearance of the student's plant after 20 days by the window.

Complete the diagram below to show the appearance of the student's plant after 20 days by the window. [1 mark]

d Explain the advantage to the plant of growing in the way that you have drawn it in part **c**.

_____

_____

_____ [2 marks]

2. Plants respond to different environmental factors because of hormones.

Which hormone is responsible for the direction of growth of roots? Tick **one** box.

☐ Adrenaline   ☐ Progesterone   ☐ Nitrate

☐ Auxin   ☐ Potassium   [1 mark]

3. Ethene is a plant hormone that causes fruit to ripen.

Higher Tier only Scientists measured the concentration of ethene found in fruit at different stages of ripeness.

The graph below shows the results.

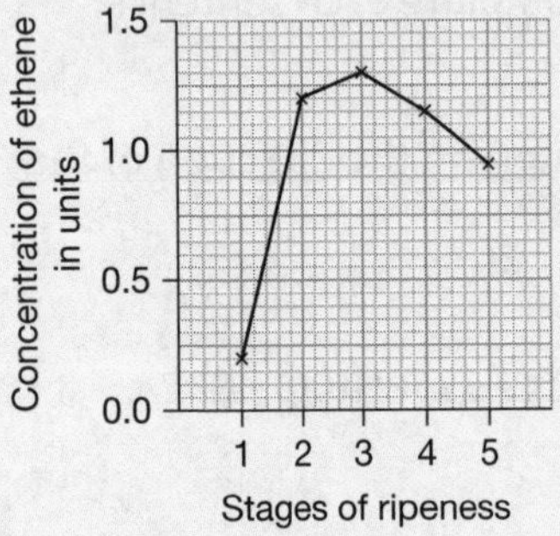

a At which stage of ripeness is there most ethene?

Stage _____   [1 mark]

b Suggest how the scientists can find out if the result for Stage 1 was an anomaly.

_____   [1 mark]

c Gibberellins are a different type of plant hormone.

Farmers growing cotton plants in cold climates sometimes soak their seeds in a solution of gibberellins before planting the seeds.

Suggest an advantage of soaking seeds in a gibberellin solution in cold climates.

_____

_____   [2 marks]

Plant hormones and their uses

1. A student grew a plant in an upright plot.

She then put the pot in a horizontal position and left the plant in the dark for two days.

The diagram shows the potted plant after two days in the dark.

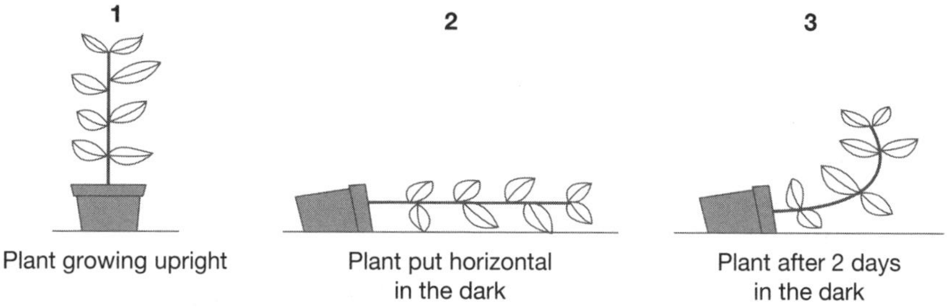

1	2	3
Plant growing upright	Plant put horizontal in the dark	Plant after 2 days in the dark

Explain fully why the plant responded in this way.

_____

_____

_____ [4 marks]

2. Match the hormones to their correct uses. Some hormones may have more than one use.

Higher Tier only

Hormones

Auxins

Ethene

Gibberellins

Uses

Promote flowering

Fruit ripening

Increase fruit size

Weedkillers

[4 marks]

3. The effect of auxin on the growth of pea plants was investigated by a group of students.

One set of plants was sprayed with auxin. Another set of plants was sprayed with water. The plants were each 60 cm tall before the investigation.

The table shows the results of the investigation.

	Height of pea plants (cm)	
	Sprayed with auxin	Sprayed with water
Plant 1	104	65
Plant 2	93	61
Plant 3	99	62
Mean		62.66

Maths **a** Calculate the mean height for the plants sprayed with auxin. Write your answer in the table.

_____ [1 mark]

b Explain why one set of plants was sprayed with water.

_____ [1 mark]

c Describe the effect of auxin on the pea plants.

_____

_____ [2 marks]

Maths

The mean height of the plants sprayed with auxin is expressed to the same number of decimal places as the mean of the plants sprayed with water. So you should round up or down to 2 decimal places.

Sexual reproduction and fertilisation

1. The offspring of a zebra and a horse is called a zorse.

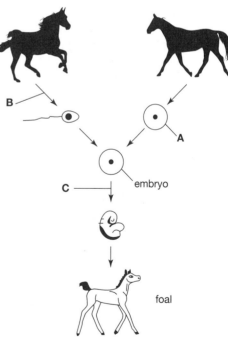

a Which technique is used to produce a zorse?
Tick **one** box.

☐ Cloning   ☐ Sexual reproduction

☐ Asexual reproduction   ☐ Mutation

[1 mark]

b Explain the appearance of the zorse. Use **both** words from the box in your explanation.

| gametes   genes |

_____

_____ [2 marks]

2. The diagram shows some of the stages of reproduction in horses.

a Name this type of reproduction.

_____ [1 mark]

b Name the type of cell labelled **A.**

_____ [1 mark]

c Name the type of cell division taking place at the stage labelled:

B: _____ [1 mark]

C: _____ [1 mark]

d When the foal grows up it will look similar to its parents. But it will **not** be identical to either parent. Explain why.

_____

_____ [2 marks]

Asexual reproduction

1. 'Walking onion' plants grow a bunch of bulblets (tiny bulbs). The bulblets start to grow and the stalks bend over with the weight of the new growth. This makes the onion plant seem to walk across the garden.

Producing plants this way is called **asexual reproduction**.

Use the words from the box to complete the following sentences.

| chromosome   clone   gamete   gene   parent |

New shoot forming from a bulblet

Bulblet

Stalk bending over

New daughter plant forming

Asexual reproduction needs only one _____. Asexual reproduction

does **not** involve production of a _____. The daughter plant is called a

_____.

[3 marks]

2. New plants can be produced using tissue culture. Tissue culture is a type of asexual reproduction.

Another method of producing new plants is by taking cuttings.

Suggest **one** advantage of using tissue culture and **not** using cuttings to produce new plants.

_____

_____

[1 mark]

3. What are the **advantages** of asexual reproduction?

_____

_____

_____

_____

[4 marks]

Cell division by meiosis

1. In which of the following would you expect meiosis to take place? Tick **two** boxes.

☐ Ovaries ☐ Uterus ☐ Bladder ☐ Testes ☐ Prostate [2 marks]

2. An animal has 36 chromosomes in each of its body cells.
How many of these chromosomes come from its male parent?

_____ [1 mark]

> **Remember**
> Half of the chromosomes come from each parent.

3. The diagram shows the chromosomes in an animal cell dividing by meiosis.

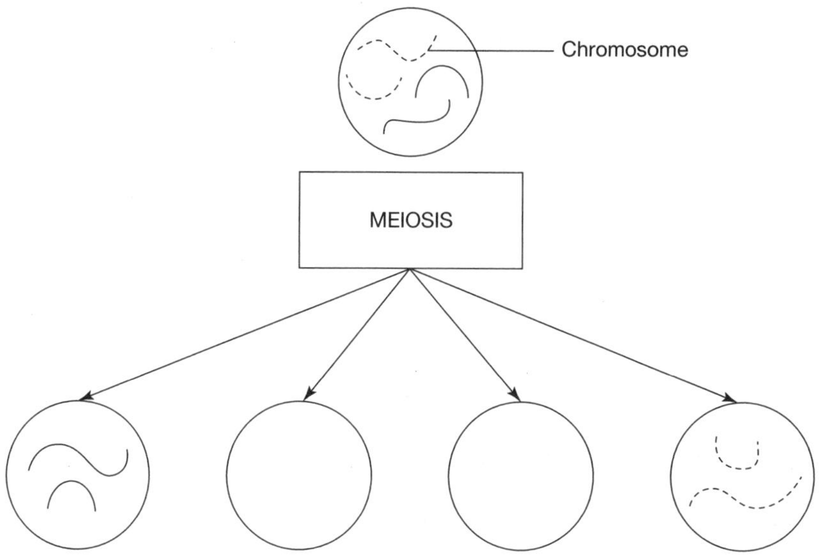

Chromosome

MEIOSIS

a Complete the diagram. Draw in the empty cells the reassorted chromosomes which would produce two **genetically different** cells. [2 marks]

b Where are chromosomes found in a cell? _____ [1 mark]

c Where in the body does meiosis occur? _____ [1 mark]

d Give **two** differences between mitosis and meiosis.

_____

_____ [2 marks]

Comparing sexual and asexual reproduction

1. The following are statements about sexual and asexual reproduction.

   For each statement, tick whether it is true or false.

	True	False
Asexual reproduction involves two parents.		
Sexual reproduction produces variation in the offspring.		
Asexual reproduction is faster than sexual reproduction.		
Sexual reproduction is time- and energy-efficient.		

   [4 marks]

2. Discuss the advantages and disadvantages of cloning compared to sexual reproduction.

   _____

   _____

   _____

   _____

   _____   [5 marks]

3. Explain the advantages of asexual reproduction in plants and animals. Below is a student's answer to this question. [6 marks]

Asexual reproduction allows the body to repair cells for growth, it has the same genetic information as the parents, there is no need for fusion of gametes. Two genetically identical daughter cells are produced.

This answer is only worth 1 mark for stating there is no need for fusion of gametes. The student missed out on a chance to gain credit for explaining why asexual reproduction would be advantageous to animals and plants. The command word 'explain' means to provide an account of the advantages of asexual reproduction. The important point to note is that a description for both animals and plants is required. A good strategy would be to provide three points for each.

DNA, genes and the genome

1. Choose words from the box to complete the sentences below.

| body | chromosomes | clones | cytoplasm | genes | nucleus | sex |

Information is passed from parents to their young, in _____ cells.

Each characteristic, e.g. fur colour, is controlled by _____. The structures that

carry information for a large number of characteristics are called _____. The

part of the cell which contains these structures is called the _____.   [4 marks]

2. Circle the correct answer.

In the nucleus of a cell, genes are part of:

chromosomes   membranes   receptors   cytoplasm   [1 mark]

3. The Human Genome Project was a study to map all the genetic information on the chromosomes of a human being.

a Explain **two** benefits of understanding a person's genome.

_____

_____   [2 marks]

Higher Tier only **b** What is the function of non-coding regions of DNA?

_____   [1 mark]

Structure of DNA

1. The diagram shows the structure of a small section of DNA.

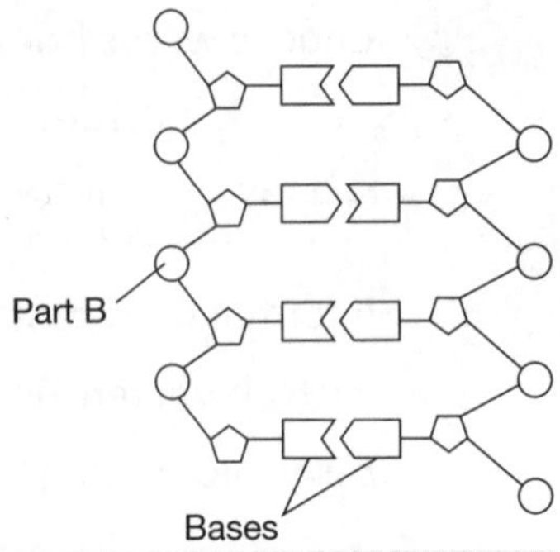

    a What is part B? _____ [1 mark]

    b What are the four bases?

    _____ [1 mark]

Higher Tier only   **c** There are four bases and they pair up in the same pairs.

    Which bases pair up together?

    _____ [2 marks]

2. A large sample of DNA was analysed and in it base G made up 28% of the number of base molecules present. Calculate the number of T base molecules present as a percentage.

Higher Tier only

You must show your working.

Maths

> **Remember**
> G pairs with C; therefore C will also make up 28% of base molecules. This leaves a total of 44% bases left (100 – (28+28) = 44). As A and T are also present in pairs, they will be half of 44 each.

_____

    Percentage of T bases = _____% [2 marks]

3. Explain the importance of the sequence of bases in DNA.

_____

_____

_____ [3 marks]

4. A DNA molecule consists of two strands coiled to form a double helix.

Describe how the two strands of a DNA molecule are linked together.

_____

_____ [2 marks]

Protein synthesis and mutations

1. A strand of DNA has a sequence of bases (A, C, G and T). What is a section of DNA which codes for **one** specific protein called?

________________ [1 mark]

2. The diagram shows part of one DNA strand.

Higher Tier only

DNA strand	G	G	C	T	A	G	T	T	G
mRNA strand									

a Complete the empty boxes to show the mRNA strand coded for by this DNA. [1 mark]

b State the maximum number of amino acids coded for by this DNA strand.

________________ [1 mark]

c Name the structure where translation occurs. ________________ [1 mark]

3. Compare coding and non-coding parts of DNA.

Higher Tier only

____

____

____ [3 marks]

4. Describe the process of protein synthesis.

Higher Tier only

____

____

____

____ [4 marks]

Inherited characteristics

1. Put a ring around the correct answer to complete each sentence below.

The alleles present in the cell are the <u>genotype / phenotype</u>.

A recessive allele is <u>always expressed / only expressed</u> if two copies are present.

If **two** alleles present are recessive, the organism is <u>heterozygous / homozygous</u>.   [3 marks]

2. Coat colour in rabbits is controlled by **one** pair of genes. The allele for black coat (N) is dominant to the allele for brown coat (n). Parent A, who has a black coat is crossed with Parent B, a brown-coated rabbit. They produced 5 rabbits with black coats and 7 with brown coats.

Complete the diagram to show how the young rabbits inherited their coat colour.

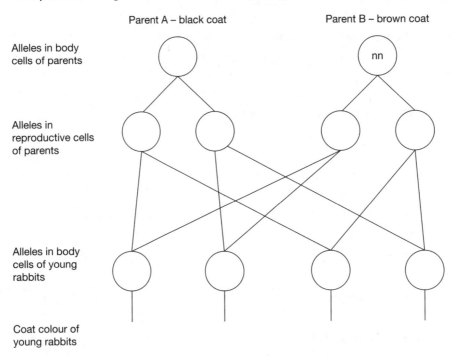

Parent A – black coat   Parent B – brown coat

Alleles in body cells of parents

Alleles in reproductive cells of parents

Alleles in body cells of young rabbits

Coat colour of young rabbits

Use the symbols N and n for the alleles.

The alleles of the brown parent have been inserted for you.   [3 marks]

3. Mice with black fur can have the genotype BB or Bb, and mice with brown fur have the genotype bb.

a Draw a Punnett square diagram to show what fur colours you would predict in the F1 offspring produced by two mice who are both Bb. [3 marks]

> **Remember**
> Place the father's alleles on the top of the Punnett square with one letter above each box. Place the mother's alleles on the left hand side of the square, with one letter in front of each box. Use capital letters for the dominant genes and lower-case letters for the recessive alleles.

b Why might your prediction of fur colour in the F1 generation **not** be proved right?

_____ [1 mark]

c Using the example of the mice coat colour to help:

(i) describe the difference between dominant and recessive alleles.

_____

_____ [2 marks]

(ii) describe the difference between alleles and genes.

_____

_____ [2 marks]

(iii) describe the difference between homozygous and heterozygous chromosomes.

_____

_____ [2 marks]

Inherited disorders

1. Haemophilia is a genetic disorder which is sex-linked.

The diagram shows a family tree.

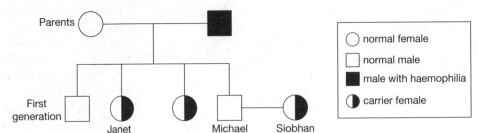

XH represents a normal X chromosome.

Xh represents an X chromosome carrying the haemophilia allele.

Y represents a Y chromosome.

  a Give the genotype of the parents.

      Father: _____   **Mother:** _____   [2 marks]

  b Give the phenotype and genotype of Janet.

      Phenotype: _____   **Genotype:** _____   [2 marks]

  c Explain how Michael does **not** have haemophilia even though his father does.

      _____

      _____   [2 marks]

Higher Tier only

  d Michael and Siobhan have children. What proportion of the children will have

      haemophilia? _____   [1 mark]

Maths

  e Why are there fewer females with haemophilia than males?

      _____

      _____   [2 marks]

2. Mutations of DNA cause some inherited disorders.

One inherited disorder is cystic fibrosis (CF). A recessive allele causes CF.

a Complete the genetic diagram. [2 marks]

Neither parent has CF. Put a circle around any children with CF.

The following symbols have been used:

D = dominant allele for **not** having CF

d = recessive allele for having CF

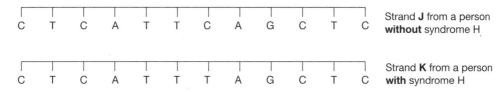

Mother

		D	d
Father	D	DD	
	d		

b Give the probability of any children having CF.

Probability of having a child with CF: _____ [1 mark]

c What is the genotype of the mother shown in the diagram in part **a**? Tick **one** box.

☐ Heterozygous ☐ Homozygous dominant

☐ Homozygous recessive [1 mark]

3. Syndrome H is an inherited condition.

People with syndrome H do **not** produce the enzyme IDUA.

The diagram shows part of the gene coding for the enzyme IDUA.

C	T	C	A	T	T	C	A	G	C	T	C

Strand **J** from a person **without** syndrome H

C	T	C	A	T	T	T	A	G	C	T	C

Strand **K** from a person **with** syndrome H

Strand **K** shows a mutation in the DNA which has caused syndrome H.

The enzyme IDUA helps to break down a carbohydrate in the human body.

The enzyme IDUA produced from Strand **K** will **not** work.

Explain how the mutation could cause the enzyme **not** to work.

_____

_____

_____

_____

_____ [5 marks]

Sex chromosomes

1. Humans have two different sex chromosomes, X and Y.

The diagram shows the inheritance of sex in humans.

		Mother	
		X	X
Father	X	XX	XX
	Y	XY	XY

   a   Circle a part of the diagram that represents an egg cell. [1 mark]

   b   Circle a part of the diagram that shows the genotype of male offspring. [1 mark]

2. A man and a woman have two sons. The woman is pregnant with a third child.

What is the chance that this child will also be a boy? Tick **one** box.

☐ 0%　　☐ 25%　　☐ 50%　　☐ 100% [1 mark]

3. In humans, sex chromosomes control whether a person is male or female.

   a   Use letters X and Y to complete the Punnett square for sex inheritance.

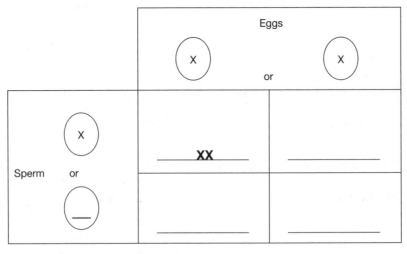

[3 marks]

A couple already have three boys.

   b   What is the probability that their next child will be a girl? _____ [1 mark]

Variation

1. Members of a clone of 'Bizzy-Lizzy' seedlings were planted at various distances from a north-facing wall. The diagram shows variation between the plants 6 weeks after planting.

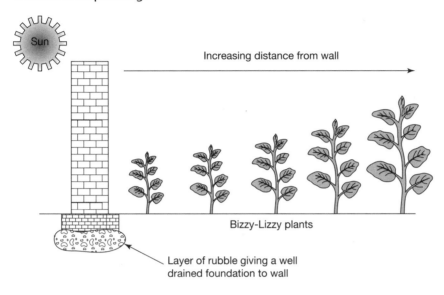

a What is meant by the term variation?

_____ [1 mark]

b Suggest **two** reasons why the plants showed variation in height after 6 weeks.

_____

_____ [2 marks]

c What type of variation is shown by the plants? Tick **one** box.

☐ Genetic ☐ Environmental ☐ Genetic and environmental [1 mark]

d Give a reason for your answer to **c**.

_____ [1 mark]

2. Explain how a population of antibiotic-resistant bacteria might develop from non-resistant bacteria.

_____

_____

_____

_____ [3 marks]

3. **a** Give **two** factors which bring about variation in humans.

1 _____

2 _____ [2 marks]

b There is large variation within a population of a species.

A student was asked to suggest **two** factors which could produce this range of variation. [2 marks]

Worked Example

Variation is because of the genes that are inherited or the environmental conditions.

This answer only gets 1 mark for correctly pointing out both genetic and environmental factors. The student could have gained an extra mark by writing about mutations causing variation in the population. Another credit-worthy suggestion is that there is a large gene pool for this population, which means a large number of combinations of genes are possible.

Evolution by natural selection

1. Draw a circle around the correct answer to complete each sentence. [3 marks]

Evolution can be explained by a theory called genetic engineering/mutation/natural selection.

This theory was suggested by a scientist called Charles Darwin/Lamarck/Semmelweiss.

This scientist said that all living things have evolved from monkeys/dinosaurs/simple life forms.

2. Many religious people **oppose** the theory of evolution. Give **one** reason why.

_____ [1 mark]

3. The picture shows a modern swordfish.

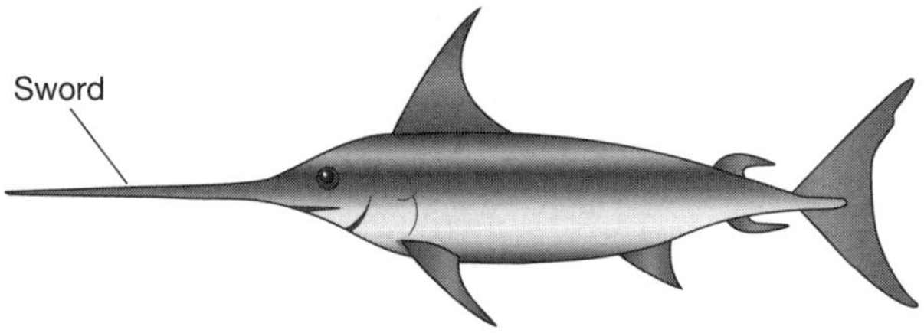

Ancestors of swordfish had shorter swords. Swordfish use their swords to injure prey. The injured prey is easier to catch. The information in the box shows one theory of how the length of the sword of swordfish changed.

> The sword grew longer as each swordfish used its sword more and more.
> Each time a swordfish reproduced, the longer sword was passed on to its offspring.
>
>
> Many generations

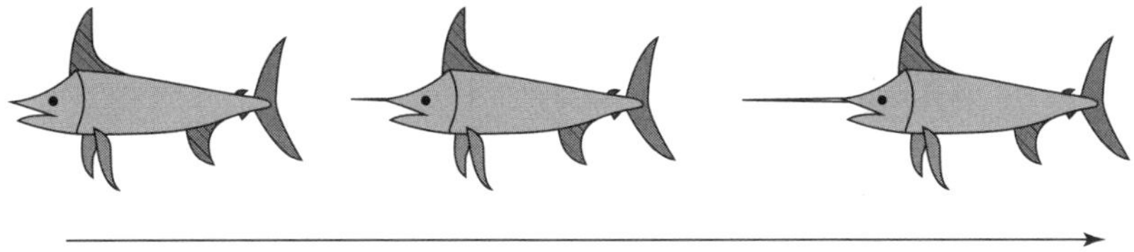

a Which scientist suggested the theory?

_____ [1 mark]

b Darwin suggested that evolution is a result of natural selection.

Describe how natural selection could result in modern swordfish developing from ancestors with short swords.

_____

_____

_____

_____ [4 marks]

4. The vole is a small, mouse-like animal. Voles found on some cold islands to the north of Scotland are much larger than voles in warmer areas such as southern France. Explain how natural selection may have caused the southern voles to be smaller. **[5 marks]**

Worked Example

Because it is warmer in the south of France, the voles there are smaller because they have less fat for insulation. More body heat can be lost if there is no insulation.

The student gains 2 marks for stating that voles in southern France have less fat on their bodies and that this can help them lose more body heat. However, the answer gives a Lamarckist explanation – as if it is the temperature of the south of France that determines the size of the vole. For a Darwinist answer, it is best to state that voles with a smaller body size will survive the warmer temperatures by helping them to lose body heat efficiently. These better-adapted animals will survive and reproduce to pass on their beneficial genes to some of their offspring.

Darwin and Wallace

1. Draw **one** line from each scientist to the description of their significant work.

Charles Darwin		Carried out breeding experiments on pea plants.
Alfred Russel Wallace		Wrote *On the Origin of Species.*
Gregor Mendel		Worked on plant defence systems.
		Worked on warning colouration in animals.

[3 marks]

2. Tick **one** box to complete each sentence.

a Darwin suggested the theory of evolution by _____ selection.

☐ artificial   ☐ natural   ☐ asexual   **[1 mark]**

b Most scientists believe that life first developed about _____ years ago. Tick **one** box.

☐ three billion   ☐ three million   ☐ three thousand   **[1 mark]**

c Darwin's theory of evolution was only slowly accepted by other people. Give **two** reasons why.

_____

_____ [2 marks]

3. Briefly explain Darwin's theory of evolution.

_____

_____

_____

_____ [4 marks]

Speciation

1. In the 1800s, Charles Darwin visited the Galapagos Islands and found many different species of finch, a type of bird.

Darwin thought that all the different finch species had evolved from **one** species of finch that had reached the islands many years before.

The diagram shows information about ten species of finch, A–J.

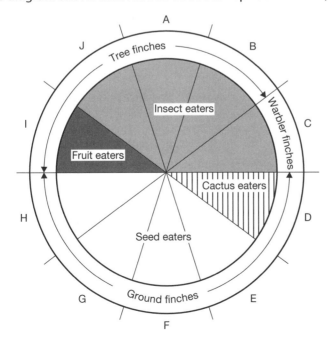

a How many of the species of finch eat insects? Tick **one** box.

☐ 4   ☐ 5   ☐ 6

[1 mark]

b Describe finch species G. Use only information from the diagram.

_____

_____

[2 marks]

2. Both white herring gulls and (Alaskan) lesser black-backed gulls are found in Britain.

White herring gulls cannot breed with (Alaskan) lesser black-backed gulls.

White herring gulls can breed with American herring gulls.

American herring gulls can breed with (Alaskan) lesser black-backed gulls.

a This type of interbreeding between different species is known as

_____.

[1 mark]

b What does this interbreeding of gulls result in? Tick **one** box.

☐ Circular species   ☐ Isolation

☐ Ring species   ☐ Speciation

[1 mark]

Synoptic **c** The binomial term for the white herring gull is *Larus argentatus*.

State the level of classification that *Larus* in the binomial name refers to.

_____

[1 mark]

Synoptic **d** Discuss how interbreeding in gulls may make classification difficult.

_____

_____

_____

[2 marks]

Synoptic **e** Gulls belong to the phylum chordata.

Explain which features of gulls enable them to be classified in a vertebrate group.

_____

_____ [2 marks]

3. Discuss the definition of the term species.

_____

_____

_____

_____

_____

_____ [6 marks]

Modern understanding of genetics

1. Mendel's experiments were published in 1866 around the same time that Darwin's *On the Origin of Species* was published. However, the link between the two did not become apparent until the 1920s.

Which explanation is correct? Tick **one** box.

☐ Scientists believed that God created variation in species.

☐ Mendel's paper was not read widely.

☐ Darwin's book was banned in the press.

☐ Scientists discredited Mendel because he was a monk.

2. The diagram shows an experiment performed by a scientist called Mendel in the 1850s. He bred pea plants which had different coloured seeds.

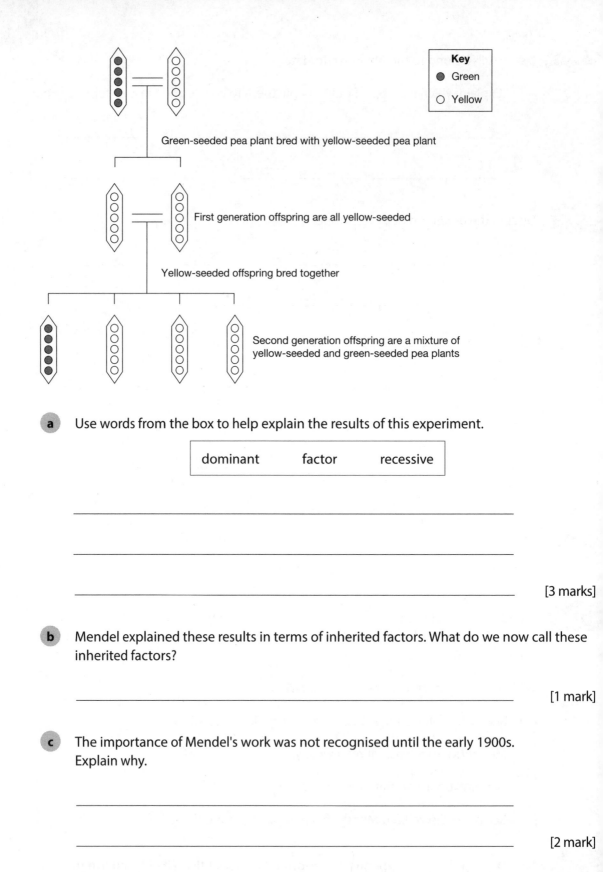

Green-seeded pea plant bred with yellow-seeded pea plant

First generation offspring are all yellow-seeded

Yellow-seeded offspring bred together

Second generation offspring are a mixture of yellow-seeded and green-seeded pea plants

Key
● Green
○ Yellow

a Use words from the box to help explain the results of this experiment.

| dominant | factor | recessive |

_____

_____

_____ [3 marks]

b Mendel explained these results in terms of inherited factors. What do we now call these inherited factors?

_____ [1 mark]

c The importance of Mendel's work was not recognised until the early 1900s. Explain why.

_____

_____ [2 mark]

Fossil evidence for evolution

1. The diagram shows how the number of species in vertebrate groups changed between 400 million and 5 million years ago. Wider blocks indicate more species.

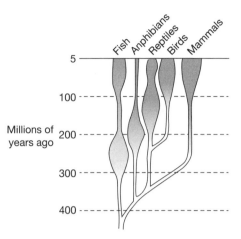

a Which group had **most** species 200 million years ago?

_____ [1 mark]

b To which group are birds **most closely** related?

_____ [1 mark]

c Complete the following sentence.

A study of fossils gives evidence for the theory of _____. [1 mark]

2. Stone tools found in layers of rock can show evidence for human evolution.

The diagram shows four locations, A, B, C and D, where stone tools were found.

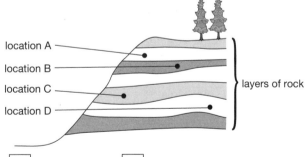

a Where were the oldest tools most likely to be found? Tick **one** box.

☐ Location A   ☐ Location B   ☐ Location C   ☐ Location D   [1 mark]

b Suggest **two** possible ways in which stone tools were used.

_____ [2 marks]

Other evidence for evolution

1. A crossbill uses its bill (beak) to force apart scales on conifer cones. It then uses its tongue to extract the seeds. If the bill is clipped it grows back again. Scientists clipped the bills of several crossbills so that their bills no longer crossed. They observed that crossbills with clipped bills took much longer to get seeds.

Use this information to suggest an explanation for the evolution of the bill. Mention the ideas of selection, competition and mutation.

_____

_____

_____

_____ [4 marks]

2. The cultivated banana is sterile and seedless. It reproduces asexually, producing shoots or suckers that develop into new plants. It is difficult to develop disease-resistant varieties of this plant.

In the 1950s, the main variety grown in banana plantations was Gros Michel. This was wiped out by Panama disease, caused by a soil fungus (*Fusarium oxysporum*). The disease spread rapidly from one plant to another and from plantation to plantation.

Following the devastation, a variety resistant to Panama disease, Cavendish, was planted and has been used ever since. However, Cavendish was susceptible to the disease Sigatoka, caused by another fungus (*Mycosphaerella fijiensis*). Only massive amounts of fungicide spray keep Sigatoka under control. It seems that as soon as a new fungicide is used, the fungus develops resistance to it.

Synoptic **a** State the genus of the fungus that causes Panama disease.

_____ [1 mark]

b Explain why Panama disease spread so quickly and wiped out Gros Michel.

_____

_____ [3 marks]

> **Remember**
> This answer requires knowledge that plants in the plantation grow close together; also the plants are clones of each other and therefore susceptible to the same diseases.

c Explain how the fungus that causes Sigatoka becomes resistant to fungicides.

_____

_____

_____

_____

_____ [6 marks]

3. Outline five types of evidence which support the theory of evolution by natural selection.

_____

_____

_____

_____

_____ [5 marks]

4. Explain how evidence from antibiotic resistance in bacteria supports the
theory of evolution. [6 marks]

A student has written the following answer to this question.

Worked Example

Bacteria evolves to get a higher tolerance or resistance to antibiotic. Therefore, antibiotic doesn't really affect bacteria. As the bacteria multiply they have a wide range of genetic variation. The bacteria carrying resistant genes lives on to reproduce.

This answer can only gain 2 marks as it does not really discuss the *way* antibiotic resistance in bacteria provides evidence for the theory of evolution. The student needs to use the idea of how bacterial resistance arises and then link that to why it would be evidence for evolution. There needs to be some indication that the student understands that the rapid reproduction cycle of bacteria shows how survival of the fittest leads to the selection of bacteria that are resistant and able to go on to produce offspring that contain their beneficial genes.

Extinction

1. Scientists believe that dinosaurs became extinct about 65 million years ago in the second greatest mass extinction.

   What do they believe caused this mass extinction? Tick **one** box.

   ☐ A change in ocean currents   ☐ Asteroid impact   ☐ Warming of the Earth

   ☐ New predators   ☐ New diseases

   [1 mark]

2. When animals die, they usually fall to the ground and decay. In 1977, the body of a baby mammoth was discovered. The baby mammoth died 40 000 years ago and its body froze in ice.

   a Explain why the body of the baby mammoth did **not** decay.

   _____

   _____ [2 marks]

   b Mammoths are closely related to modern elephants. Mammoths are now extinct. What does 'extinct' mean?

   _____ [1 mark]

   c Scientists are still looking for a definitive explanation for the extinctions of mammoths.

   Select **two** possible reasons for their extinction.

   ☐ Over-hunting by humans   ☐ Volcanic activity   ☐ Asteroids

   ☐ Global dip in temperature   ☐ Global warming   [2 marks]

Selective breeding

1. Most cows produce milk with a fat content of 3.4%. Cow S produces milk with a fat content of 1.2%. Only cow S has the gene to produce this low-fat milk.

The diagram shows how the farmer plans to develop more cows like cow S.

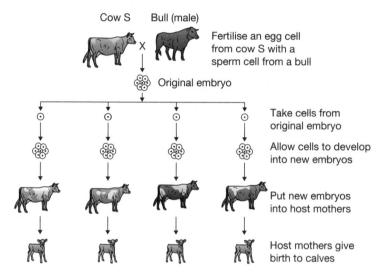

a An egg cell from cow S is fertilised by a sperm cell. This is sexual reproduction.

What is the scientific name for sex cells such as egg cells and sperm cells?

_____ [1 mark]

b After fertilisation, cells taken from the original embryo develop into new embryos.

Which part of the host mother's body is each new embryo put into?

_____ [1 mark]

c Why are calves born to all the host mothers **genetically identical** to each other?

Tick **one** box.

☐ They are formed from the same original embryo.

☐ They have the same host mother.

☐ They have the same two parents. [1 mark]

d What term describes the method of producing calves shown here?

Tick **one** box.

☐ Adult cell cloning ☐ Embryo transplantation ☐ Genetic modification

[1 mark]

e Why are the calves born to the host mothers **not** genetically identical to cow S?

_____ [1 mark]

2. Some cats are selectively bred so that they do **not** cause allergies in people.

a Suggest **two other** reasons why people might selectively breed cats.

_____

_____ [2 marks]

b Describe **one** problem inbreeding causes.

_____ [1 mark]

c Many people have breathing problems because they are allergic to cats. The allergy is caused by a chemical called Fel D1. Different cats produce different amounts. A cat is bred so that it does **not** produce Fel D1 and does **not** cause an allergic reaction.

Explain how the cat has been produced using selective breeding.

> **Command words**
> The command word 'explain' means to describe an account of and, in this question, you need to provide an account of the process of selective breeding.

_____

_____

_____

_____ [4 marks]

Genetic engineering

1. Genetic engineering involves modifying the genome of an organism by introducing a gene from another organism to give a desired characteristic.

Why are bacterial cells genetically engineered? Tick **one** box.

- [ ] To be resistant to diseases.
- [ ] To produce useful substances.
- [ ] To overcome inherited disorders.
- [ ] To produce many offspring.
- [ ] To become resistant to herbicides.

[1 mark]

2. Crops with modified genes are called genetically modified (GM) crops.

Why are some people concerned about GM crops? Tick **two** boxes.

- [ ] Pollen from GM crops may be transported to neighbouring crops.
- [ ] Not all plant cells take up the foreign gene.
- [ ] Herbicide-resistant crops may kill non-target organisms.
- [ ] Some GM crops can resist insect attack.
- [ ] GM crops can help achieve global food security.

[2 marks]

3. The diagram shows a technique used in genetic engineering.

Higher Tier only

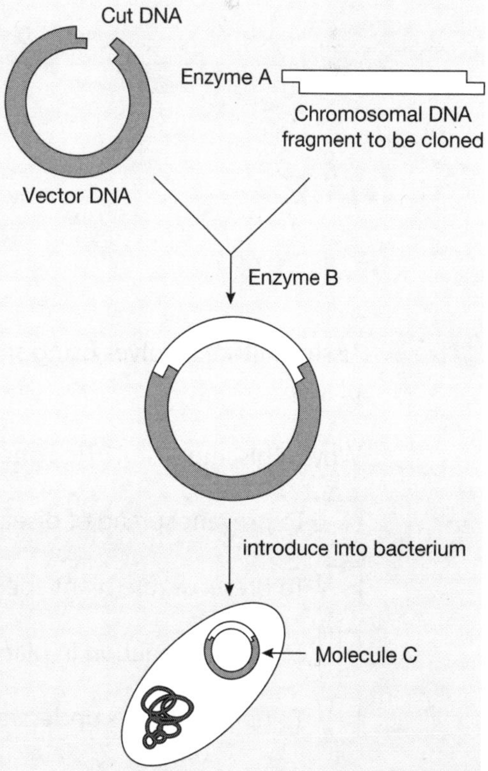

a Suggest why enzyme A is used to cut **both** the vector DNA and the chromosomal DNA fragment.

_____

_____ [2 marks]

b What is the function of enzyme B?

_____ [1 mark]

Cut DNA

Enzyme A

Chromosomal DNA fragment to be cloned

Vector DNA

Enzyme B

introduce into bacterium

Molecule C

c Trials have been done to genetically modify cauliflowers to make their leaves greener.

'Green genes' were introduced into cauliflower cells by either attaching them to part of a cauliflower virus (rendered harmless) or to a bacterial plasmid.

Suggest **three** reasons why there are concerns about this technology.

_____

_____

_____ [3 marks]

4. **a** Describe how the plasmid can be used to genetically modify a bacterial cell to contain a human gene.

Higher Tier only

_____

_____

_____ [3 marks]

b Suggest how a named product from genetically modified (GM) bacteria can benefit humans.

_____ [1 mark]

Cloning

1. Tissue culture involves using small groups of cells from part of a plant to grow identical new plants.

Why is this important? Tick **one** box.

☐ To prevent spread of disease in plants.

☐ To preserve rare plant species.

☐ To ensure variation in plants.

☐ To help scientists understand how to clone animals. [1 mark]

2. The diagram shows how an immature egg could be used **either** to produce cells to treat some human diseases **or** to produce a baby.

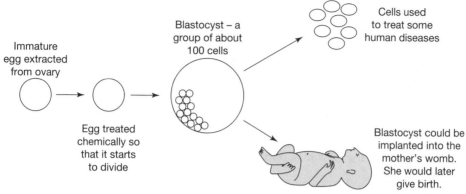

Immature egg extracted from ovary

Egg treated chemically so that it starts to divide

Blastocyst – a group of about 100 cells

Cells used to treat some human diseases

Blastocyst could be implanted into the mother's womb. She would later give birth.

Scientists can use this technique to produce cells to treat some human diseases, but **not** to produce babies. Using the diagram, suggest an explanation for this.

_____

_____

_____

_____ [4 marks]

3. To produce a herbicide-resistant crop plant, the herbicide-resistance gene is obtained from a herbicide-resistant plant. It is then inserted into the cells of a tissue culture from the crop plant.

a Which structure in a cell carries the genes? _____ [1 mark]

b How is the herbicide-resistance gene cut out of this structure?

_____ [1 mark]

Classification of living organisms

1. *Russula silvicola* is a multicellular organism that does **not** have chlorophyll.

a *Russula silvicola* belongs to which kingdom? Tick **one** box.

☐ Plantae   ☐ Fungi   ☐ Prokaryotes   ☐ Protoctista   [1 mark]

b *Russula silvicola* is the binomial name of this mushroom.

Draw **one** straight line from each part of the binomial name to its classification.

Binomial name

Russula

silvicola

Classification

species

family

phylum

genus

order

[1 mark]

c State **two** characteristics of the kingdom Plantae.

_____

_____   [2 marks]

d Vertebrates belong to the kingdom Animalia. Use words from the box to complete the following sentence.

chordata	chromosome	backbone	prokaryote	protoctista	cell

Vertebrates are members of the phylum _____
and most have a _____ running the length of the body.   [2 marks]

2. Bacteria are classified as prokaryotes. State **two** characteristics of prokaryotes.

_____

_____   [2 marks]

3. The diagram shows one model of the relationship between some animals.

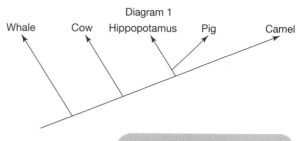

Diagram 1

Whale   Cow   Hippopotamus   Pig   Camel

a Complete the sentence. The diagram

is an evolutionary _____.

[1 mark]

b Which **two** of the animals are most closely related?

_____ [1 mark]

c The diagram below shows a **more recent** model of the relationship between the animals.

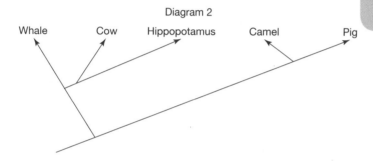

Diagram 2

Whale   Cow   Hippopotamus   Camel   Pig

> **Remember**
>
> The tips of the tree represent the species and the nodes on the tree represent the common ancestors of the species. In the tree above, hippopotamus and pig are closely related to each other since they share a common ancestor.

Suggest **one** reason why scientists have changed the model of animal relationships. Tick **one** box.

☐ More powerful computers.   ☐ New evidence from fossils.

☐ New species discovered.

[1 mark]

Habitats and ecosystems

1. Use words from the box to complete the sentences.

| respiration | germination | pollination | warmth | photosynthesis |
| | interdependence | shelter | dependency | |

The plants and animals in an ecosystem depend on each other in many different ways. Plants

carry out _____, helping to regulate the concentration of oxygen and carbon

dioxide in the atmosphere. Many animals depend on plants for food and _____.

Some plants rely on insects such as bees for _____ and seed dispersal. The way

living organisms interact and rely on each other to survive is called _____.

[4 marks]

2. Which of the following statements **best** describes a community? Tick **one** box.

☐ All the organisms that live in a country.

☐ One species of organism living in an ecosystem.

☐ All the living organisms that interact within the same ecosystem.

☐ The non-living parts of an ecosystem. [1 mark]

3. What is meant by the term 'population'?

_____ [1 mark]

4. The diagram shows the different levels of organisation found within an ecosystem.
Draw **one** line from each label to the matching level on the diagram.

community

ecosystem

population

individual

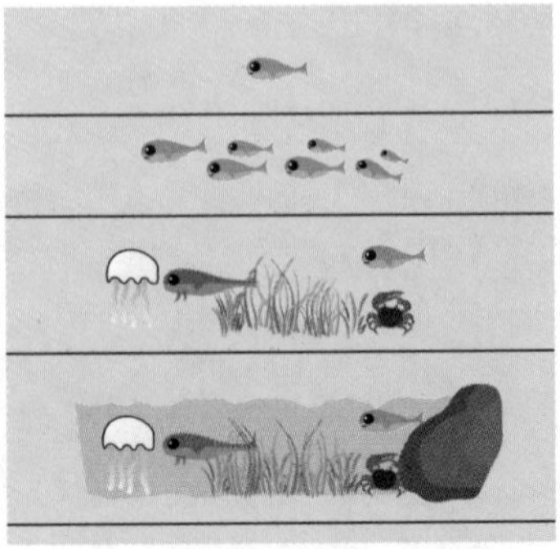

[4 marks]

5. For an ecosystem to be stable and self-supporting, it must have an external source of energy which is usually the Sun or an artificial light source. Explain why this is.

_____

_____

_____

_____ [4 marks]

Food in an ecosystem

1. Add the following labels to the food chain.

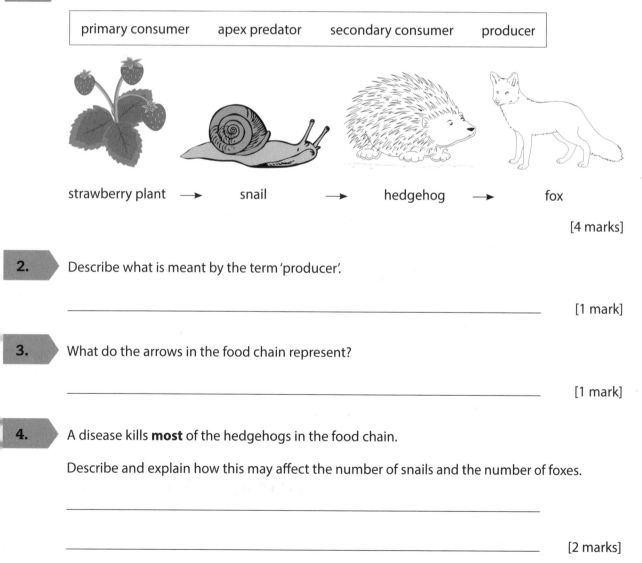

| primary consumer | apex predator | secondary consumer | producer |

strawberry plant → snail → hedgehog → fox

[4 marks]

2. Describe what is meant by the term 'producer'.

_____ [1 mark]

3. What do the arrows in the food chain represent?

_____ [1 mark]

4. A disease kills **most** of the hedgehogs in the food chain.

Describe and explain how this may affect the number of snails and the number of foxes.

_____

_____ [2 marks]

Biotic and abiotic factors

1. Circle **two** biotic factors from the list.

| light | pathogens | temperature | moisture | predators | wind |

[2 marks]

2. Explain what is meant by the term 'abiotic factor'.

_____ [1 mark]

3. List **three** abiotic factors that might affect the distribution of species in a pond.

_____

_____ [3 marks]

4. Which example shows a relationship between both an abiotic and a biotic factor in an ecosystem? Tick **one** box. [1 mark]

☐ Algae being eaten by a fish.   ☐ A tree removing a gas from the air.

☐ Water carrying a rock downstream.   ☐ A flower providing food for an aphid.

5. Egg wrack is a seaweed that grows on rocky shores. Egg wrack grows on parts of the shore that get covered by water twice a day when the tide comes in.

The graph shows the distribution of egg wrack on a rocky shore. A student was asked to look at the graph and answer the questions below.

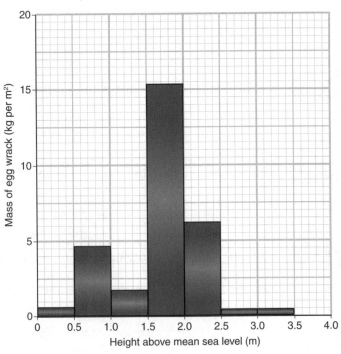

a At what height interval above mean sea level is the largest mass of egg wrack found? [1 mark]

Height interval: <u>1.5 metres</u>

> This would not get the mark. The graph shows the mass of egg wrack in height intervals so the answer is 1.5–2.0 m.

b Describe what happens to the distribution of egg wrack above 2 metres above sea level. Suggest an explanation for the pattern you describe. [2 marks]

The distribution decreases.

This might be because any higher than 2 metres it would be uncovered by sea water for too long.

> This answer is correct. As the command word 'suggest' is used, the student has correctly used 'might' in the response. 'Suggest' questions often have more than one possible answer so words such as might, could, or 'I think that' are appropriate.

6. The graph shows a model predator–prey cycle for foxes and rabbits.

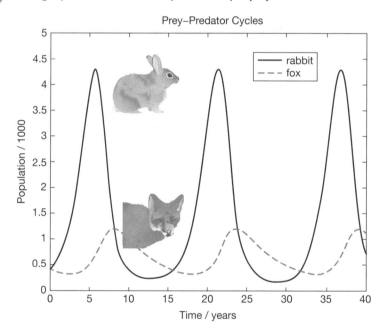

Prey–Predator Cycles

Describe and explain the pattern shown by the graph.

_____

_____

_____

_____

_____

_____

_____

_____ [6 marks]

Adapting for survival

. . . .

1. Draw **one** line from each animal to show how it is structurally adapted to its environment.

		Thick fur and blubber
Camel		
		Long sticky tongue
Polar bear		
		Large surface area to volume ratio
Toad		
		Scales

[3 marks]

2. Describe the **difference** between a structural and a behavioural adaptation.

_____

_____ [2 marks]

3. The plant *Urtica dioica*, commonly known as the stinging nettle, is covered in long thin hollow hairs that contain stinging chemicals. Suggest how this is an adaptation for survival.

_____ [1 mark]

4. Bacteria living in deep sea vents can survive temperatures between 40°C and 80°C. What is the name given to organisms that can survive in extreme environments?

_____ [1 mark]

5. African elephants are the world's largest land mammal. They live in desert environments.

Suggest how the following features help the African elephant to survive there.

Large ears: _____

_____

Tusks: _____

_____ [2 marks]

Measuring population size and species distribution

1.

Required
practical

A student investigates the effect of trampling on the number of buttercup plants in the school field. She compares an area that is well trampled to an area that is untrampled. Then she samples the buttercups using a 20-metre transect line and a 1 m² quadrat.

Describe, step by step, how the student could do this, taking readings at 5-metre intervals.

_____

_____

_____

_____

_____

_____ [5 marks]

2. The table shows the data collected in the trampled area.

Quadrat sample number	Number of buttercups in trampled area
1	0
2	3
3	0
4	1
5	4

Maths

a Calculate the mean, modal and median number of buttercups for the five quadrat samples.

_____

Mean number of buttercups: _____

Modal number of buttercups: _____

Median number of buttercups: _____   [3 marks]

> **Maths**
> Make sure you are clear about the difference between mean, median and mode. Think of a way to help you remember the difference. The mean is a bit 'mean' because you have to add up all the numbers and then divide the sum by how many numbers were added. Median sounds like medium or the number in the middle of the data. MOde is the MOST frequent number. They both have 'mo' at the beginning.

b The last quadrat placed on the untrampled field was under the shade of a large tree.

Suggest and explain how the tree might affect the number of buttercups.

_____

_____   [2 marks]

Cycling materials

1. Use the words from the box to complete the sentences below.

carbon	cycled	nitrogen	silver	physical	leached	biotic

Nutrients are chemical elements that all plants and animals require for growth. They include

water, _____ and _____. Each nutrient is _____
from the physical environment into living organisms, and then recycled back to the

_____ environment. This movement of nutrients is a vital function of the

ecology of an area.   [2 marks]

2. The diagram shows the carbon cycle.

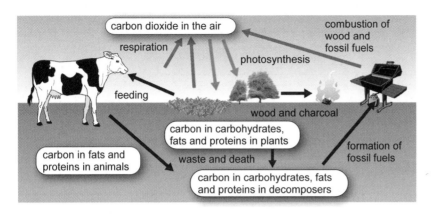

a Give the name of a process that **removes** carbon dioxide from the air.

_____ [1 mark]

b Give the name of **two** processes that release carbon dioxide into the air.

_____ [2 marks]

c Dead organisms are decomposed by microorganisms. Why is this an important part of the carbon cycle?

_____ [1 mark]

d Why does the recycling of carbon and other nutrients take longer in waterlogged soils?

_____

_____ [2 marks]

3.

Maths

In 1995, the amount of carbon released into the atmosphere by burning fuels was 5.3 billion tonnes. In 2015, this had increased to 7.4 billion tonnes.

Calculate the percentage increase in the amount of carbon released. Give your answer to 2 decimal places.

_____

Percentage increase = _____ %   [2 marks]

4. Explain why the water cycle is important to living organisms.

_____

_____

_____ [3 marks]

Decomposition

1. Use the words from the box to complete the sentences below.

> absorb   accumulate   toxins   digest   protozoa   fungi   enzymes   recycle

Decay is an essential life process, which helps to _____ food and

_____ materials so they can be used again. Bacteria and _____

are the main groups of decomposers. They release _____ to break down
compounds, so that they can absorb the nutrients. [2 marks]

2. Explain why nutrient recycling takes longer in acidic soils than in neutral soils.

_____ [1 mark]

3. Many food products last longer when stored in the fridge. Explain why this is.

_____

_____ [2 marks]

4. Which **two** of the following statements about biogas are true?

☐ Biogas is produced naturally in marshes, septic tanks and sewers.

☐ 50–75% of biogas is carbon dioxide.

☐ Biogas generators provide a cheaper fuel source.

☐ Biogas production only occurs at very low temperatures. [2 marks]

5. A class investigates the effect of temperature on the rate of decay of fresh milk by measuring pH change. Their method is shown below.

Required practical

1. Add 6 drops of phenolphthalein to a test tube; then add 5 cm³ of milk and 7 cm³ of sodium carbonate solution.

2. Place test tube in water bath until contents reach same temperature.

3. Add 1 cm³ of lipase into the test tube and start the stop clock.

4. Stir the contents of the test tube until the solution loses its pink colour and record the time.

5. Repeat steps 1–4 for a range of different temperatures.

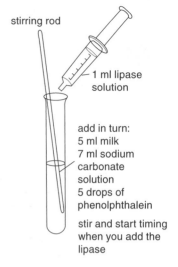

stirring rod

1 ml lipase solution

add in turn:
5 ml milk
7 ml sodium carbonate solution
5 drops of phenolphthalein

stir and start timing when you add the lipase

a Explain why the phenolphthalein changes colour from pink to colourless. [2 marks]

Worked Example

When the fat in the milk is broken down by the lipase, fatty acids are made.

> This is a good, clear response which would gain both marks.

The fatty acids lower the pH of the mixture causing the colour change.

b Increasing temperatures from 0°C to 45°C reduces the time taken for the lipase to break down the fat in milk. However, over 45°C, the time taken increases and in some cases the lipase does not work at all.

Explain why the temperature affects the rate of decay of fresh milk in this way. [4 marks]

Because increasing the temperature increases the rate of reaction by increasing the collision rate between the enzyme and substrate molecules. This means the enzyme-controlled reactions that cause decay are increased and the rate of decay of milk increases up until 45°C.

> It is more scientific to say the enzyme is 'denatured' by high temperatures. To gain full marks, the student would need to explain this in more detail. The protein structure of the enzyme is denatured by temperatures above 40°C causing the molecule to lose its shape, which deactivates the enzyme. As a result, the enzyme-controlled reactions that cause decay cannot occur.

After 45°C the rate of enzyme reactions decreases as temperature increases until, at some point, the reaction stops altogether.

This is because at high temperatures the enzyme is killed by the heat.

Changing the environment

1.

Higher Tier only

Draw **one** line from each environmental change to its potential impact.

Environmental change	Potential impact
Sinking of land bridge joining two continents.	Animals hibernate longer than normal.
Low temperatures and food shortage.	Animals cannot move between continents.
Global warming causes sea to become more acidic.	Shells of calcareous organisms dissolve and become thinner.

[3 marks]

2.

Higher Tier only

Which of the following are examples of natural environmental change? Tick **two** boxes.

☐ Higher average temperatures caused by sunspot activity.

☐ Decreased marine biodiversity due to dredged seabeds.

☐ Increased atmospheric carbon dioxide and sulfur dioxide due to burning of fossil fuels.

☐ Increased atmospheric carbon dioxide and sulfur dioxide due to volcanic activity.

[2 marks]

3.

Higher Tier only

The Aral Sea has been steadily shrinking since the 1960s after the rivers that fed it were diverted by irrigation projects. This caused environmental changes such as:

- an increase in salt concentration of the sea;
- a decrease in the oxygen concentration of the water;
- higher sea temperatures.

Suggest and explain how these changes could have affected the distribution of plants and fish in the Aral Sea.

Remember
This type of question requires you to apply your knowledge in a new context. As the question says 'suggest', there will be more than one possible answer; and as long as you back up your suggestions with scientific explanations, you will have a good chance of picking up marks.

_____

_____

_____

[3 marks]

Effects of human activities

1. Define what is meant by the term 'biodiversity'.

_____

_____ [1 mark]

2. Give **one** reason why biodiversity is beneficial for an ecosystem.

_____ [1 mark]

3. As the human population increases, more land is being used to grow crops. Often one crop is grown over a huge area. What are the negative effects of this change in land use on our ecosystems? Tick **two** boxes.

☐ There is less food available for insect pollinators such as bees.

☐ There is less acid rain.

☐ Habitats are created.

☐ Habitats are destroyed. [2 marks]

4. Peat bogs take thousands of years to form. What is the main reason peat bogs are being destroyed? Tick **one** box.

☐ To produce garden compost. ☐ To clear land for houses.

☐ To produce charcoal. ☐ To prevent the spread of malaria. [1 mark]

5. The rainforests in many countries are under threat from deforestation.

Give **two** reasons why tropical rainforests are being destroyed.

_____

_____ [2 marks]

6. The pie chart below shows what happens to the domestic waste we produce in the UK.

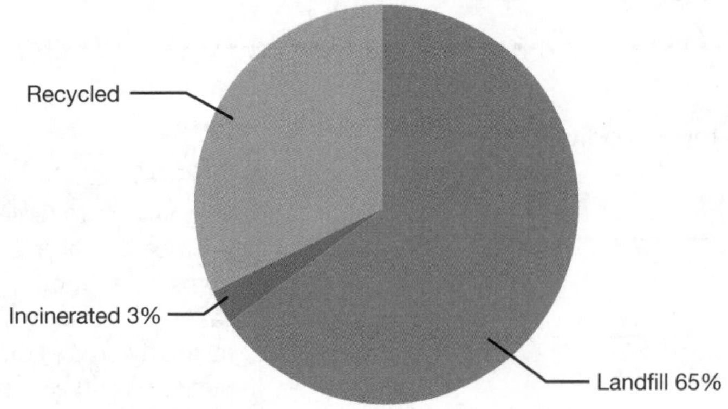

Recycled
Incinerated 3%
Landfill 65%

Maths

It is a straightforward calculation to find out a missing percentage from a pie chart. The 'per cent' means 'out of 100' so remember that all the numbers in a pie chart must add up to 100.

Maths **a** Calculate what percentage of waste gets recycled.

____

Percentage of waste recycled = __________________ % [1 mark]

b Describe **two** ways a landfill site can reduce biodiversity of the area.

____

____ [2 marks]

7. Describe and explain the consequences of deforestation on the ecosystem.

____

____

____

____ [4 marks]

Global warming

7

1. Which **two** of the following gases contribute to global warming?

oxygen	carbon dioxide	methane	nitrogen	sulfur dioxide

[2 marks]

2. The gases that cause global warming occur naturally in the atmosphere, but human activities have increased the level of these gases.

List **two** human activities that have increased the level of these gases.

_____

_____ [2 marks]

3. The graph shows temperature difference compared to 1880 global average temperature between 1880 and 2005.

Describe the pattern shown by the graph. Evaluate to what extent the data provides evidence for global warming. [4 marks]

Worked Example

The graph shows that the temperature has fluctuated but overall there is an increase in global temperature.

The graph clearly shows an overall trend of increasing global temperatures. This is strong evidence that global warming is happening as the temperature increase is more than what has been observed in the past.

Overall, the evidence for global warming shown by the graph is quite strong.

The student has correctly described the general pattern shown by the graph and stated the overall trend.

The student has remembered to make a concluding remark based on the strength of the evidence.

129

4. Describe the possible consequences of global warming.

_____

_____

_____

_____ [4 marks]

Maintaining biodiversity

1. Monoculture is the growing of **one type** of crop in a field. How can farms growing monocultures limit the impact of this style of farming on the ecosystem? Tick **one** box.

☐ By removing all hedgerows and trees.

☐ By replanting hedgerows.

☐ By trimming hedgerows.

☐ By adding fertilisers to hedgerows. [1 mark]

2. Farmers are encouraged to reintroduce field margins. Explain how this increases biodiversity.

_____

_____ [2 marks]

3. Many households in the UK now regularly recycle household paper waste such as newspapers.

Explain how this helps protect our ecosystems.

_____

_____

_____ [3 marks]

4. A tree replanting programme claims that replanting trees helps to offset CO_2 emissions from human activities. Evaluate to what extent this claim is true.

_____

_____

_____ [2 marks]

5. Many conservation programmes aim to protect endangered species.

An example is the International Gorilla Conservation Programme in Africa.

Why are conservation programmes such as this beneficial to a country? Tick **two** boxes.

☐ They keep damage to food chains and food webs to a minimum.

☐ They require a lot of funding.

☐ They can attract tourists and therefore benefit the economy.

☐ They prevent endangered species from breeding. [2 marks]

6. The Mangrove Action Project is an organisation that is involved with the conservation and restoration of mangrove forests around the world.

A student's answer to the following question is given below. Suggest **two** difficulties organisations such as the mangrove Action Project may face in trying to conserve and restore the mangrove forests. [2 marks]

Worked Example

The local people might rely on the mangrove forests for food so might not want it to be protected.

Local people or building companies might not know about the importance of the mangrove so might think it doesn't matter if it gets destroyed.

Mangroves are complicated ecosystems that need experts to be involved with restoration and finding experts may be difficult and expensive.

This answer gives three difficulties, which are all correct answers, but the question only asks for **two** so the student would only get 2 marks and has wasted time writing about three issues.

Biomass in an ecosystem

1. Use the words from the box to complete the sentences.

wet	dry	number	energy	food	mass

Pyramids of biomass show the _____ of organisms at different trophic levels.

The biomass is calculated using the _____ mass of the organisms at each level.

The biomass contains stored _____ so shows how much energy there is at

each level.

[3 marks]

2. This is a food chain found in a garden:

1 rose bush ⟶ 40 greenflies ⟶ 5 ladybirds

Maths The biomass of each organism is shown in the table.

Organism	Biomass (g)
1 rose bush	200
1 greenfly	0.5
1 ladybird	1

Use the information in the table to construct a pyramid of biomass for this food chain.

_____

Remember

If you are asked to draw a pyramid of biomass you must draw it to scale. In this example you need to start by calculating the total biomass at each trophic level. Each bar should get narrower as you go up a level. Remember to label each bar with the name of the organism.

[3 marks]

3. The total mass of the organisms at each level in the pyramid **decreases** as you move up the pyramid. Explain why.

_____

_____

_____ [3 marks]

4. The table shows the amount of energy transferred at each trophic level in a lake.

Maths

Trophic level	1	2	3	4
Name of organism	waterweeds	tadpoles	minnow	pike
Energy transferred to next level kJ/m²/year	80000	7900	760	63
Efficiency of energy transfer /%	–		9.6	8.3

Calculate the efficiency of energy transfer between the waterweeds and tadpoles. Give your answer to 1 decimal place.

_____

Efficiency of energy transfer = _____% [2 marks]

Maths

To calculate energy efficiency, you need to use this formula:

Efficiency =

$$\frac{\text{energy available after the transfer}}{\text{energy available before the transfer}} \times 100$$

Food security

··

1. Which statement **best** describes what is meant by the term 'food security'? Tick **one** box.

◻ Keeping food safe. ◻ Providing nutritious food to all children.

◻ Providing food during times of conflict or war. ◻ Having enough food to feed a population. [1 mark]

2. Which of the following are factors that could affect food security? Tick **three** boxes.

◻ Increasing birth rate

◻ New pests that affect farming

◻ More people growing their own food

◻ Increasing costs of pesticides

◻ More people becoming vegetarian

◻ Use of hybrid crop varieties [3 marks]

3. Suggest and explain how a drought could threaten food security.

_____

_____ [2 marks]

4. Explain what is meant by the term 'sustainability'.

_____ [1 mark]

5. Cod fish stocks in the Atlantic Ocean are being depleted due to overfishing.

Describe **two** practices that could help cod fish stocks to be maintained.

_____

_____ [2 marks]

6. Chickens reared for meat production are called broiler chickens.

They are often farmed intensively and thousands of chickens are kept close together in large sheds.

Give **one** advantage and **one** disadvantage of rearing chickens in this way.

Advantage: _____

Disadvantage: _____ [2 marks]

Role of biotechnology

1. Use the words from the box to complete the sentences.

sustainable   ethical   non-living   decreasing   increasing   processed   living   nutritious

Biotechnology is the use of _____ organisms to make products that can

improve the quality of life and meet the demands of the _____ population.

Food biotechnology could help us find a more _____ way of feeding the world

population by producing higher yields and more _____ food.   [2 marks]

2. Golden rice is a variety of rice that has been genetically engineered to contain vitamin A.

Which of the following is an advantage of golden rice? Tick **one** box.

☐ It can help prevent night blindness caused by vitamin A deficiency.

☐ The rice is a golden colour.

☐ It is more expensive.

☐ It can help prevent scurvy caused by vitamin C deficiency.   [1 mark]

3. For many years, insulin was obtained by purifying it from the pancreas of cows and pigs slaughtered for food. This was time-consuming and expensive. This also raised ethical issues for people with diabetes who could not use pigs insulin because of religious beliefs or vegetarianism.

Insulin is now made by genetically engineered microbes. The genetically modified bacteria are grown in large fermentation vats containing all the nutrients needed for growth. This allows human insulin to be produced in large quantities and then purified. This form of insulin is absorbed more rapidly than animal-derived insulin and acts more quickly.

Evaluate the **advantages** and **disadvantages** of using biotechnology to produce insulin.

Literacy

The command word 'evaluate' means you should use the information supplied, as well as your own knowledge and understanding, to write about the advantages and disadvantages of using biotechnology. At the end you should say whether it is a good idea based on the points you have raised.

_____

_____

_____

_____

_____ [6 marks]

Plant and animal cells (eukaryotic cells)

1. Nucleus – controls the cell's activities; [1 mark] chloroplast – where photosynthesis occurs; [1 mark] cell membrane – controls what enters and leaves the cell; [1 mark] cell wall – for support and protection; [1 mark] cytoplasm – where the cell's activities occur [1 mark]

2. Top: cell membrane; [1 mark] left: nucleus; [1 mark] bottom: cytoplasm. [1 mark]

3. **a** B, C, A [1 mark]

   b As a stain [1 mark] so he can see the organelles. [1 mark]

   c To prevent air bubbles getting trapped under coverslip. [1 mark]

Bacterial cells (prokaryotic cells)

1. Smaller; simple; single; bacteria. [4 marks]

2. A – cell wall; B – cell membrane; C – cytoplasm; D – chromosomal DNA. [4 marks]

3. **a** The cytoplasm. [1 mark]

   b The nucleus. [1 mark]

4. 2/1000 = 0.002 mm. [1 mark]

5. $0.002 = 2 \times 10^{-3}$. [1 mark]

Size of cells and cell parts

1. (Smallest) 1 – ribosome; 2 – mitochondrion; 3 – sperm cell; 4 - egg cell; 5 – nerve cell from giraffe's neck. [5 marks]

2. ×400. [1 mark]

3. 50 mm. [1 mark]

4. **a** $50 \times 1000 = 50\,000$ μm. [1 mark]

   b 50 000/25 = ×2000. [1 mark]

5. ~1 μm (i.e. one-sixth the size of the cell, which is 6 μm). [1 mark]

The electron microscope

1. How much bigger the image of a sample is relative to its actual size. [1 mark]

2. The smallest distance between two points that can still be seen as two points. [1 mark]

3. It has enabled scientists to observe sub-cellular structures in much more detail and therefore increased our understanding. [1 mark]

4. Advantages: You can obtain good quality images of the internal structure of the cells; they have a better resolution than light microscopes; they have higher magnification than light microscopes.

   Disadvantages: They're very expensive; specialist training is needed to use them; specimen must be dead and prepared in a vacuum. [4 marks]

Growing microorganisms

1. Binary fission. [1 mark]

2. 3 hours. [1 mark]

3. **a** It contains all the nutrients and water needed for the microorganism to grow/reproduce. [1 mark]

   b To make sure they are not contaminated with bacteria. [1 mark]

4. **a** Antibiotic 2: radius = 7 mm; [1 mark] area = 153.86 mm² [1 mark]

   b Antibiotic 1 has a larger zone of inhibition; [1 mark] so more of the *E.coli* have been killed [1 mark]

Cell specialisation and differentiation

1. Unspecialised, differentiate, cilia, specialised. [4 marks]

2. Differentiation [1 mark]

3. They contain many mitochondria. [1 mark]

4. Small size of red blood cells mean they can travel through small capillaries; bi-concave shape gives a large surface area/surface area: volume ratio for absorbing oxygen; contain haemoglobin to carry oxygen; no nucleus so more room for haemoglobin to carry oxygen. [4 marks]

Cell division by mitosis

1. Mitosis produces two new cells that are identical to each other, and to the parent cell. [1 mark]

2. 46 [1 mark]

3. Top row of diagram – the cell grows. The number of sub-cellular structures, e.g. mitochondria,

increases. [1 mark] Middle of diagram – the DNA replicates to form two copies of each chromosome. One set of chromosomes is pulled to each end of the cell and the nucleus divides. [1 mark] Bottom row – the cytoplasm and membrane divides and two identical cells are formed. [1 mark]

4. **a** Three. [1 mark]

   b 3 × 23 hours 18 minutes = 69 hours, 54 minutes; [1 mark] convert to minutes 69 × 60= 4140 + 54 = 4194 minutes. [1 mark]

5. In the nucleus. [1 mark]

6. Number of sub-cellular organelles increases; cell grows. [1 mark]

Stem cells

1. Differentiate, embryos, bone marrow. [3 marks]

2. Any type of human cell. [1 mark]

3. Meristem tissue. [1 mark]

4. It is wrong to destroy life/embryo cannot give permission. [1 mark]

5. Umbilical cord. [1 mark]

6. Nerve cell. [1 mark]

7. Risks of using stem cells: Unknown long-term side effects; chance of rejection if stem cells are not from the same person; person may need to take anti-rejection medication for the rest of their lives. [2 marks]

   Benefits of using stem cells: Low risk of rejection if cells are from the same person; can be used for treatment of cancer/Parkinson's/diabetes, etc. [2 marks]

   Evaluation – student answer – suitable statement to support or reject use of stem cells. [1 mark]

Diffusion

1. Molecules from an area of high concentration to an area of low concentration. [1 mark]

2.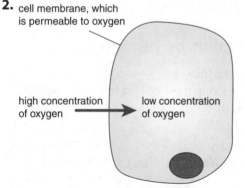

cell membrane, which is permeable to oxygen

high concentration of oxygen   low concentration of oxygen

[1 mark]

3. Any **two** from: difference in concentration; temperature; surface area of the membrane. [2 marks]

4. Red blood cells are too big to fit through the capillary walls. [1 mark]

5. If the air is warmer, the molecules of carbon dioxide have more energy [1 mark] and move faster, so the rate of diffusion is faster. [1 mark]

6.

Level 3: The response gives a clear and detailed explanation of the role of diffusion in gas exchange. The response is well structured.	
Level 2: The response gives some explanation of the role of diffusion in gas exchange. The response has some structure and some of the points are linked together.	
Level 1: The response gives basic information about the role of diffusion in gas exchange. The answer may lack structure and points are not linked together.	
Indicative content	
• When you breathe in, the concentration of oxygen molecules in the alveoli is higher than in the capillaries surrounding the alveoli. • This creates a concentration gradient and therefore… • Oxygen molecules diffuse through the thin walls of your alveoli and into the capillaries. • Carbon dioxide concentration in the capillaries surrounding the alveoli is greater than the air breathed in/air in alveoli. • This creates concentration gradient. • Carbon dioxide diffuses from blood into the alveoli and out of the lungs.	

[6 marks]

Exchange surfaces in animals

1. Surface area of 3 × 3 × 3cm cube = 54 cm^2; [1 mark] volume = 27 cm^3; [1 mark] SA:V = 2:1. [1 mark]

2. Cell A [1 mark] because it has a larger surface area. [1 mark]

3. In a single-celled organism the surface area to volume ratio is big/high [1 mark] so sufficient nutrients such as oxygen can diffuse in. [1 mark] A large multicellular organism, like a human, has a much smaller/lower surface area to volume ratio [1 mark] so it need specialised organs like lungs to exchange materials. [1 mark]

4. It has villi to give a large surface area to maximise absorption. [1 mark] It has thin walls to provide a short diffusion path. [1 mark] It has an efficient blood supply/surrounded by many capillaries. [1 mark]

Osmosis

1. Water, dilute, concentrated. [3 marks]

2. It is a membrane or barrier that allows some molecules or substances to cross, but not others. [1 mark]

3. a To avoid weighing excess water on the surface of the potato. [1 mark]

   b To allow time for osmosis to take place. [1 mark]

   c Both axes correctly labelled; points plotted correctly; correct line of best fit. [3 marks]

   d Accept between 11.5% and 13.5%. [1 mark]

   e Yes, because at this concentration there was no change in mass [1 mark] because concentration in boiling tube and potato cells was the same so no osmosis took place. [1 mark]

Active transport

1. Lower, higher, against, energy. [4 marks]

2. The soil contains a very dilute concentration of mineral ions compared to the root hair, so the ions need to be moved against a concentration gradient requiring active transport. [2 marks]

3. Active transport works against a concentration gradient whereas diffusion works along a concentration gradient. Active transport requires energy from respiration whereas diffusion does not require energy. Both are forms of transport that move substances. [4 marks]

Digestive system

1.

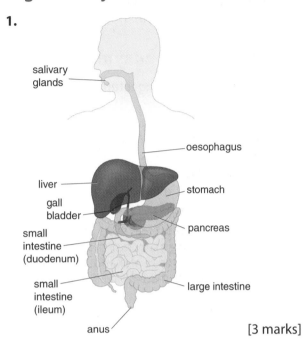

salivary glands

oesophagus

liver

stomach

gall bladder

pancreas

small intestine (duodenum)

small intestine (ileum)

large intestine

anus

[3 marks]

2. An organ system in which several organs work together to break down and absorb food. [1 mark]

3. To break down food so it can be absorbed and used by the body. [1 mark]

4. Physical digestion is the physical breaking up of food into smaller pieces; chemical digestion is the breakdown of food into small molecules by enzymes so they can be absorbed by the blood. [2 marks]

Digestive enzymes

1. Small, bloodstream, proteins, respiration. [4 marks]

2. Amylase is produced in the salivary glands [1 mark] and breaks down starch into glucose. [1 mark]

Middle row: protease. [1 mark] Bottom row: lipids. [1 mark]

3. Benedict's test – carbohydrates – sugars. [1 mark] Biuret test – proteins. [1 mark] Iodine test – carbohydrates – starch. [1 mark]

4. a Grinding – to increase the surface area. [1 mark] Adding distilled water – to make a solution. [1 mark]

b Biuret test: Add a few drops of biuret solution into the milk solution; the solution will turn from blue to purple/violet colour if protein is present. [2 marks]

Factors affecting enzymes

1. a The iodine will no longer turn blue - black. [1 mark]

b The temperature of the water bath is much easier to control. [1 mark]

c When the sample is tested at regular intervals to find out if the starch has been broken down. [1 mark]

d 40 degrees [1 mark]

e The rate of reaction reaches a maximum [1 mark] because many fast-moving substrate molecules enter and fit easily into the active site. [1 mark]

Heart and blood vessels

1. a Clockwise from top left: pulmonary artery, aorta, pulmonary vein, vena cava. [4 marks]

b Arrow into pulmonary vein. [1 mark]

c Arrow out of aorta. [1 mark]

2. A pacemaker is a group of cells in the right atrium of the heart. [1 mark]

Artificial pacemakers can be used to correct irregularities in the heart rate. [1 mark]

3. The walls are thin [1 mark] and permeable. [1 mark]

4. Any **six** points from: arteries have thicker walls and a smaller lumen than veins; [1 mark] veins have valves; [1 mark] both vessels carry blood around the body; [1 mark] the arteries carry oxygenated blood away from the heart, [1 mark] whereas the veins carry deoxygenated blood towards the heart (except the pulmonary artery); [1 mark]; arteries have pressure and a pulse [1 mark] but the veins carry blood under lower pressure and have no pulse. [1 mark] [6 marks]

Blood

1. Red blood cells – transport oxygen around the body. [1 mark]

White blood cells – protect the body from infection. [1 mark]

Platelets [1 mark] – help the clotting process at wound sites.

2. Any **three** from: hormones, antibodies, nutrients (glucose, amino acids, minerals, vitamins), waste substances (carbon dioxide, urea). [3 marks]

3. If they are unwell/fighting an infection/cancer. [1 mark]

4. It gives it a large surface area [1 mark] to allow greater absorption of oxygen. [1 mark]

5. a 3575 cm^3 (55/100 × 6 500 cm^3). [1 mark]

b 5.0×10^6. [1 mark]

Heart–lungs system

1. Trachea, bronchus, bronchiole, alveoli. [1 mark]

2. The blood flows in two circuits [1 mark] – one from heart to lungs and one from heart to rest of body. [1 mark]

3. Any **four** points from: the spherical shape gives a large surface area to volume ratio, which enables efficient diffusion of gases; [1 mark] the wall of alveoli is very thin so gases do not have far to diffuse; [1 mark] each alveolus is surrounded by a network of capillaries/good blood supply so oxygen is constantly moved into the blood and carbon dioxide moved into the lungs; [1 mark] this means gas exchange happens at the steepest concentration gradient possible; [1 mark] alveoli surfaces are moist so gases dissolve, allowing efficient diffusion. [1 mark]

Coronary heart disease

1. This disease is not passed from one person to another/is not infectious. [1 mark]

2. C, A, D, B [4 marks]

3. It may result in backflow [1 mark] so blood is pumped much less efficiently; [1 mark] **or** oxygenated and deoxygenated blood may mix [1 mark] so oxygen is not pumped as efficiently. [1 mark]

4. Advantage: no rejection. [1 mark]

Disadvantage: patient needs anti-clotting drugs for rest of life or artificial valve can damage red blood cells. [1 mark]

5. Stent: opens up an artery to allow blood to supply the heart muscle with glucose and oxygen for respiration. [1 mark]

Statins: stop the liver producing as much cholesterol, so less narrowing of arteries. [1 mark]

6. Any **two** from: Change diet so less cholesterol/fat; exercise more; stop smoking; stop drinking alcohol. [2 marks]

7. The benefits are that with a heart transplant the person will live longer and have a better quality of life because they will have more energy and strength with a new heart. The risks are that the person has to have surgery, which is dangerous if it goes wrong. The person could bleed to death or get an infection from the operation. The person would also have to take anti-rejection drugs which might have side effects. The person might have to wait a long time for a donor heart because there is a shortage of heart donors, so they might die waiting for a new heart. Overall, the benefits outweigh the risks because the person will be alive longer with a heart transplant. The person would probably die sooner if they did not have the transplant. [5 marks]

Risk factors for non-infectious diseases

1. Tobacco use, physical inactivity, unhealthy diet and the harmful use of alcohol. [1 mark]

2. Any **three** from: gender; age; diet; whether the person smokes or not; alcohol consumption; genetics. [3 marks]

3. Many diseases are caused by an interaction of a number of factors. [1 mark] It is therefore difficult to collect data that prove causal mechanism. [1 mark]

4. a Accept 2500–3000. [1 mark]
   b More older people suffer coronary heart disease than younger people. [1 mark]
   c Women live longer. [1 mark]

Cancer

1. Strict, mutation, tumour, lifestyle. [4 marks]

2. Any **three** from: smoking, drinking alcohol, being overweight, an unhealthy diet, lack of exercise, overexposure to ionising radiation, viruses. [3 marks]

3. Viruses living in cells can be the trigger for certain cancers. [1 mark] As a tumour grows, cancer cells can detach and spread to other parts of the body. [1 mark]

4. Chemical or other agent that causes cancer. [1 mark]

5. Any **two** from: A benign tumour is slow-growing, a malignant tumour is faster; a benign tumour often has a clear border, a malignant does not necessarily; a benign tumour is not cancerous, a malignant tumour is; a benign tumour rarely spreads, a malignant tumour spreads to other body tissues easily. [2 marks]

Leaves as plant organs

1. Clockwise from the top of the diagram: palisade cell, spongy mesophyll cell, stoma, guard cell. [4 marks]

2. Because it is a group of tissues performing a function (photosynthesis). [1 mark]

3. Xylem [1 mark] and phloem. [1 mark]

4. The shoots of a plant. [1 mark]

5. Broad leaves: give large surface to absorb maximum amount of light. [1 mark]

   Palisade cells: contain many chloroplasts/arranged end-on to absorb maximum amount of light. [1 mark]

   Thin and transparent upper epidermis: allows maximum light to pass through to palisade cells. [1 mark]

Transpiration

1. Light intensity, temperature, wind. [3 marks]

2. The movement of water through the plant and leaves. [1 mark]

3. $5 \times 60 = 300$ seconds; [1 mark] $9/300 = 0.03$. [1 mark]

4. a Any **two** from: temperature, air movement/wind, light, humidity. [2 marks]
   b Plant A lost more water ($252 - 239 = 13g$) than plant B ($137 - 129 = 8g$). [1 mark] The rate of transpiration was higher in plant A/the plant with broad flat leaves. [1 mark] This is because a broad flat leaf loses more water than a needle due to larger surface area/more stomata for water to diffuse from. [1 mark]

Translocation

1. The movement of dissolved sugars around the plant. [1 mark]

Answers

2. Some is stored and some is used for respiration. [1 mark]

3. They have a large surface area to maximise the absorption of water. [1 mark]

4.

Level 3: The response gives a clear and detailed comparison of the structures and functions of xylem and phloem. The response is well structured.	5–6
Level 2: The response gives some comparisons of the structures and functions of xylem and phloem. The response has some structure.	4–5
Level 1: The response gives basic information about the structure and function of xylem and phloem but no or limited comparisons. The answer lacks structure.	1–2
Indicative content Structure: Both xylem and phloem are found in vascular bundles. Phloem cells are elongated, thin-walled, living cells that form tubes. Xylem tubes are made from dead cells that are strengthened by lignin and form hollow tubes. Phloem contains sieve plates. Xylem does not contain sieve plates. Function: Phloem transports dissolved sugars from the leaves to the rest of the plant. Transport of substances in the phloem can be in any direction. Xylem transports water and minerals from the roots to the stem and leaves. Transport of water and minerals is in one direction. Phloem is transport mechanism for translocation. Xylem is transport mechanism for transpiration.	

Microorganisms and disease

1. Communicable: Any **one** from: measles; mumps; rubella; colds; flu; impetigo; any other infectious disease. [1 mark]

   Non-communicable: Any **one** from: diabetes; coronary heart disease; stroke; cancer. [1 mark]

2. Viruses – flu; protists – malaria; fungi – Athlete's foot; bacteria – food poisoning. [4 marks]

3. Yes; many women with cervical cancer have HPV16 (18, 31). [2 marks] **or** No; few women with cervical cancer have HPV 6 or 11. [2 marks] The other marks for any **two** points from: HPV does not mean causation because it may be caused by another factor/due to coincidence; did not study HPV in healthy women; having cancer may cause susceptibility to HPV; does not add up to 100%; not all women with cancer have HPV.

Viral diseases

1. Viruses live inside cells. [1 mark]

2. Dead/inactive/weakened pathogen/virus. [1 mark]

3. Any **two** from: birds fly; more birds than pigs; human contact with birds more likely. [2 marks]

Bacterial diseases

1. Bacteria can infect plants and animals. [1 mark]

2. **a** D. [1 mark]

   b Largest zone of clearance/more bacteria killed. [1 mark]

3. Pain when urinating [1 mark]; yellow discharge. [1 mark]

4. Antibiotics; [1 mark] condoms/abstinence. [1 mark]

Malaria

1. Protists. [1 mark]

2. **a** Liver. [1 mark]

   b Vector. [1 mark]

3. Draining stagnant water pools: Mosquitoes lay eggs on still water; [1 mark] removing water will prevent breeding mosquitoes. [1 mark]

Using mosquito nets: Mosquitoes bite humans for a blood meal; [1 mark] if an infected person is bitten the disease is transmitted to a non-infected person at the next meal. [1 mark]

Human defence systems

1. White blood cells: produce antimicrobial substances; Stomach acid: kills the majority of pathogens that enter via the mouth; platelets: form scabs which seal the wound. [3 marks]

2. Diagram showing ingestion of group of viruses. [2 marks]

3. Hairs in the nose trap larger microbes/dust particles; [1 mark] goblet cells produce mucus; [1 mark] sticky mucus traps microbes; [1 mark] ciliated epithelium/cilia beat to waft mucus away. [1 mark]

Vaccination

1. Lives inside cells; inactive; antibodies. [3 marks]

2. a 25. [1 mark]

b 0%. [1 mark]

c No; [1 mark] as the percentage of children being vaccinated with MMR decreased, the number of children who developed autism increased. [1 mark]

3. (Flu) viruses frequently mutate into new strains; [1 mark] antigens on pathogen are changed; [1 mark] memory lymphocyte not able to recognise new antigen; [1 mark] new vaccines need to be made for flu/understanding that only some viruses mutate. [1 mark]

Antibiotics and painkillers

1. Antibiotics – kill bacteria by interfering with the process that makes bacterial cell walls; [1 mark] Painkillers – relieve symptoms of infection. [1 mark]

2. a Bacteria mutate/there is variation in bacteria; [1 mark] leading to bacteria that survive the antibiotic; [1 mark] these bacteria go on to breed. [1 mark]

b Animals do not waste energy overcoming illness; [1 mark] treated animals do not infect other animals. [1 mark]

3. Antibiotics can only kill bacteria; [1 mark] flu is caused by a virus not bacteria. [1 mark]

4. Cannot kill viral/fungal pathogens/protists; [1 mark] specific antibiotics for specific bacteria; [1 mark] emergence of resistant bacterial strains. [1 mark]

Making and testing new drugs

1. To check they work effectively; to check the right dose; to make sure they are safe to use. [2 marks]

2. Cells or tissues. [1 mark]

3. Heart drug digitalis – foxgloves; painkiller aspirin – willow trees; anti-malarial quinine – tree bark; antibiotic penicillin – mould. [2 marks]

Monoclonal antibodies

1. Myeloma. [1 mark]

2. Hybridomas. [1 mark]

3. Any **one** from: in research for finding or identifying specific molecules/measuring other hormones/to treat diseases. [1 mark]

4. True: an advantage of using monoclonal antibodies is that healthy body cells are not affected. [1 mark] Monoclonal antibodies create more side effects than expected. [1 mark]

False: monoclonal antibodies are produced in humans. [1 mark] Monoclonal antibodies cannot be used to treat cancer. [1 mark]

5. Urine is applied to one end, then it travels along the stick. There are hCG antibodies in the reaction zone. The hCG molecules in the reaction zone are attached to blue dye to make them visible. When they get to the result window, hCG molecules will attach to immobilised antibodies and since they also have the dye attached, there will be a line visible in the result window. The result is further confirmed when the unattached hCG molecules travel to the control window, where they attach to the immobilised antibodies there. [3 marks]

Plant fungal diseases

1. Fungi. [1 mark]

2. Any **two** from: refer to gardening manual or website; use testing kits; laboratory identification. [2 marks]

3. a Any **three** from: fungus penetrates (mesophyll) cells/intercellular spaces; irreversible structural changes in affected cells (accept damaged cell membranes); cells cannot photosynthesise/make food. [3 marks]

b Any **four** from: fungus produces spores; spores released in wet, humid conditions/when it rains or the plants are watered; spores dispersed by wind; optimal temperature for fungal growth (24°C)/wet, hot conditions needed for spores to germinate; symptoms start to appear on leaves 3–10 days after infection; spores produced throughout growing season; spores survive on dropped leaves/in soil. [4 marks]

c The disease is caused by fungus that produces spores, so it is really important to make sure that the affected leaves and stems are removed immediately and burned. If the infected plant is allowed to remain untreated, the spores can be spread by rain or wind. In addition, fungicides can help kill the fungus. Also, infected parts of the plant should not be composted as spores can survive and re-infect other rose plants. [4 marks]

4. Antibodies obtained from plasma of animal/rabbit; after it has been injected with the plant virus/or isolated plant pathogen antigen. [2 marks]

Other plant diseases

1. Cell wall; (waxy) cuticle. [2 marks]

2. Disease is communicable/can be spread by infected tools. [1 mark]

3. The virus makes the plant produce less chlorophyll and this means less photosynthesis. The plant needs the glucose produced during photosynthesis to grow. [2 marks]

4. a Lack of magnesium; add magnesium to the soil/magnesium-containing plant food/fertiliser. [2 marks]

b Lack of nitrates; add nitrates to the soil/nitrate-containing plant food/fertiliser. [2 marks]

Plant defence responses

1. Layers of dead cells around stems: to prevent pests from entering living cells underneath; waxy leaf cuticle: to prevent pathogens entering the epidermis; cellulose cell walls: to prevent pathogens entering cells. [3 marks]

2. Stinging hairs; stops herbivores eating them; less of the plant is damaged. [2 marks]

3. Mechanical (top row); chemical (middle row); physical (bottom row). [3 marks]

4. Tricks butterflies into not laying eggs; to prevent the caterpillars eating/damaging the plant. [2 marks]

Section 4: Photosynthesis and respiration reactions

Photosynthesis reaction

1. Leaves, light, chloroplasts. [3 marks]

2. Carbon dioxide, oxygen. [2 marks]

3. Endothermic. [1 mark]

4. Respiration. [1 mark]

5. Photosynthesis is the reaction that produces glucose. Glucose is the building block for all the tissues that make up plants/producers. Animals rely on plants/producers or other animals that eat plants for energy. [2 marks]

Rate of photosynthesis

1. Low light intensity; low carbon dioxide concentration; low temperatures (also accept low amount of chlorophyll). [3 marks]

2. a

Level 3: The response gives a clear description of a method with apparatus that would produce valid results. A description of how the rate of photosynthesis is measured is included.	5–6
Level 2: A method involving pondweed and varying light intensity is given. A description of what is measured, or at least one control variable is included.	4–5
Level 1: The response includes simple statements relating to relevant apparatus or the method involving pondweed and light.	1–2

Indicative content

- description of how the apparatus would be used.
- use of ruler to measure distance of light from beaker/pondweed.
- reference to varying distance of light from pondweed.
- accept alternative methods to alter light intensity.
- measure number of bubbles/volume of gas produced.
- same length of time.
- reference to control of temperature.
- reference to control of carbon dioxide in water.
- do repeats and calculate a mean.

b 42.3, 31.3, 22.7. [3 marks]

c 1. Bubbles may be of different sizes. [1 mark]
2. It may be difficult to count bubbles if there are lots of them. [1 mark]

d As the light intensity decreases, the rate of photosynthesis also decreases. [1 mark]

3. 0.0025. [1 mark]

4. Quarter the intensity. [1 mark]

Limiting factors

1. The plants/algae in the pond will have been photosynthesising all day/since sunrise. Photosynthesis produces oxygen so oxygen concentrations will have increased throughout the day. [2 marks]

2. a Between A and B the rate of photosynthesis increases linearly with carbon dioxide concentration, because carbon dioxide is needed for photosynthesis, so the more there is, the faster the rate. Between B and C the rate does not increase because other factors such as light intensity become limiting. [4 marks]

b Yes, because the concentration of carbon dioxide is the limiting factor up until about a concentration of 15% of carbon dioxide in the air. [1 mark]

3. Increased carbon dioxide. [1 mark] Increased temperature. [1 mark]

Uses of glucose from photosynthesis

1. Starch, storage, growth, respiration. [4 marks]

2. Plant cells respire all the time, but some also carry out photosynthesis when light is available. [1 mark] Only some plant cells can carry out photosynthesis; some, such as root hair cells, do not. [1 mark]

3. From the starch stored in the potato tuber. [1 mark]

4. The part of the potato plant above the soil can photosynthesise and therefore produce glucose for energy. [1 mark]

5. Because starch is insoluble and therefore better for storage. Glucose is soluble. [1 mark]

6. Because nitrate ions are needed to form amino acids, which are needed to make proteins. [1 mark] Proteins are required for healthy growth. [1 mark]

Cell respiration

1. Glucose; aerobically; anaerobically; mitochondria. [4 marks]

2. Respiration releases energy from glucose. [1 mark]

3. Oxygen; water. [2 marks]

4. Any **two** from: movement; keeping warm; chemical reactions to build larger molecules; active transport; cell division. [2 marks]

5. Because energy is transferred to the surroundings during the reaction. [1 mark]

6. Amino acids join together to make proteins; glucose molecules join together to make glycogen. [2 marks]

7. The carbohydrate provides the glucose needed for respiration. [1 mark] The runner's muscle cells will use lots of energy to contract during the race, so a good supply of glucose will enable the muscles to respire at a faster rate. [1 mark]

Anaerobic respiration

1. Without oxygen. [1 mark]

2. Lactic acid. [1 mark]

3. Normally we have enough oxygen for aerobic respiration to take place. [1 mark] Aerobic respiration is preferable as it produces more energy/is more efficient. [1 mark]

4. To begin with, his muscle cells respire aerobically because they have enough oxygen. [1 mark] After several minutes of sprinting his circulatory system is not able to provide enough oxygen for aerobic respiration in his muscle cells. [1 mark] The cells run out of oxygen so they switch to anaerobic respiration. [1 mark]

5. Ethanol + carbon dioxide. [2 marks]

6. Manufacture of bread and alcohol. [2 marks]

7. Yeast cells produce ethanol, whereas muscles produce lactic acid. [1 mark] Yeast produces carbon dioxide, muscle cells do not. [1 mark] Both produce little energy compared to aerobic respiration. [1 mark]

Response to exercise

1. Breathing volume, oxygenated, glucose, carbon dioxide. [4 marks]

2. They work less efficiently. [1 mark]

3. Because the body needs to get rid of the lactic acid that has built up, which needs extra oxygen/oxygen debt. [1 mark] By continuing to breathe heavily, a person can take in the extra oxygen needed to react with the accumulated lactic acid and remove it from the cells. [1 mark]

4. a B. [1 mark]
   b A. [1 mark]
   c C. [1 mark]
   d Because the oxygen debt is the amount of oxygen needed during exercise minus the amount of oxygen absorbed. [1 mark]

Section 5: Automatic control systems in the body

Homeostasis

1. Carbon dioxide; water. [2 marks]

2. Brain/hypothalamus. [1 mark]

3. 37°C. [1 mark]

4. False; true; true; false; true. [5 marks]

5. Lungs – carbon dioxide; [1 mark] kidneys – urea/ any other substance in urine (not glucose); [1 mark] skin – water/salt. [1 mark]

The nervous system and reflexes

1. a Receptor. [1 mark]
   b Sensory neurone. [1 mark]
   c Motor neurone. [1 mark]
   d Effector/muscle. [1 mark]

2. a 0.02 [1 mark]
   b Time taken for impulse to travel through gaps in the nerve cell/synapses. [1 mark]

3. Any **two** from: drop the ruler from the same height each time; let the ruler drop without using any force; same type/weight of ruler; thumb should be same distance from the ruler each time at the start; use the same hand to catch the ruler each time; carry out the experiment with the lower arm resting in the same way on the table. [2 marks]

4. No indication beforehand when the colour will change/you might be able to tell when the person is about to drop the ruler; measurement of time is more precise (than reading from a ruler)/resolution (of computer timer) is higher. [2 marks]

The brain

1. Cerebral cortex; cerebellum; medulla. [2 marks]

2. Medulla; cerebral cortex; cerebellum. [3 marks]

3. Brain/person not aware of pain/stimulus/ can't feel; possibility of (permanent/serious) damage. [2 marks]

4. Cerebellum. [1 mark]

The eye

1. The radial fibres in the iris contract. [1 mark]

2.

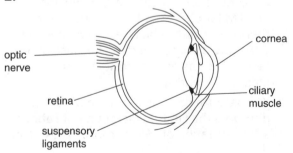

[5 marks]

3. Rods; cones. [2 marks]

4. Rods are sensitive to low light intensity so they help us to see at night-time. [1 mark]

5. Any **five** from: light enters cornea; refracted; through pupil; onto lens; refracted further; to focus; on retina; converted to chemical signals; by rods and cones; (travel through) optic nerve to brain. [5 marks]

Seeing in focus

1. The shape of the lens can change. [1 mark]

2. **a** Short-sightedness/myopia. [1 mark]

   b Light does not focus on the retina; the lens bends the light so that light focuses on the retina. [2 marks]

3. Any **two** from: contact lenses; laser surgery; artificial lenses. [2 marks]

4. **a** The ciliary muscles contract; the suspensory ligaments loosen; the lens is then thicker and refracts light rays strongly. [3 marks]

   b The ciliary muscles relax; the suspensory ligaments are pulled tight; the lens is then pulled thin and only slightly refracts light rays. [3 marks]

5. Any **four** from: short-sightedness/only able to see objects a short distance away; eyeball too long; cornea too sharply curved; image falls short of retina; corrected by concave lens. [4 marks]

Control of body temperature

1. Evaporation of water; body temperature. [2 marks]

2. **a** Blood cooled by ice; cooled blood cools brain. [2 marks]

   b Impulses/electrical signals from brain to skin; vessels/skin surface vessels/capillaries will constrict/sweat glands less active/hairs become erect; therefore, less heat lost by skin. [3 marks]

3. Muscles release energy as heat; blood flowing through muscles heated; increased blood temperature sensed by centre in brain; impulses to skin blood vessels; particularly overlying muscles used in exercise to dilate; increased surface flow in these regions; gives pattern shown on thermographs. [6 marks]

Hormones and the endocrine system

1. **a** Blood. [1 mark]

   b Glands. [1 mark]

2. Pituitary (gland); adrenal (gland). [2 marks]

3. **a** Pituitary [1 mark]

   b Regulates secretion of other glands. [1 mark]

4. **a** Pituitary (gland); thyroxine (accept thyroid hormone); adrenal (gland); oestrogen. [4 marks]

   b The pituitary gland produces thyroid-stimulating hormone which acts on the thyroid gland causing it to release thyroxine. It also produces the hormone FSH that makes the ovaries release oestrogen. [6 marks]

Controlling blood glucose

1. **a** Patrick. [1 mark]

   b Lethargy/thirst. [1 mark]

   c To convert glucose/remove glucose from the blood; their pancreas is unable to produce insulin. [2 marks]

2. Too much glucose removed from blood; fainting/coma. [2 marks]

3. Glucagon is secreted; converts stored glycogen into glucose; glucose released into the bloodstream. [3 marks]

Maintaining water balance in the body

1. **a** 1.5 [1 mark]

   b 1/3 [1 mark]

   c More sweat produced; less urine produced. [2 marks]

2. Urea. [1 mark]

Water and nitrogen balance in the body

1. Amino acids. [1 mark]

2. Hypothalamus. [1 mark]

3. Any **four** from: amino acids deaminated in liver; to form ammonia; ammonia is toxic; immediately converted to urea; dissolved in blood (plasma); transported by blood (to be excreted by kidney). [4 marks]

4. Any **six** from: ADH produced by hypothalamus; stored in pituitary; hypothalamus detects concentrated blood; ADH released from pituitary; travels in blood (to kidney tubules); kidney tubules become more permeable to water; water is reabsorbed into blood; small volume/more concentrated urine; water level in blood falls back to normal. Accept the converse argument. [6 marks]

Hormones in human reproduction

1. Ovaries; testosterone. [2 marks]

2. Ovary; uterus (womb); fertility. [3 marks]

3. FSH causes eggs to mature and stimulate ovaries to produce oestrogen; LH stimulates the egg to be released. [2 marks]

Hormones interacting in human reproduction

1. a LH. [1 mark]

   b LH production is stimulated. [1 mark]

   c Any **two** from: Placenta development; maintain blood supply; supply nutrients/remove waste products. [2 marks]

2. Any **six** from: Oestrogen levels are low in the early part of the cycle; oestrogen levels increase prior to ovulation; after ovulation, oestrogen levels drop; from day 1 – 14 progesterone levels are low; progesterone levels rise after ovulation; hormone levels drop if the ovum is not fertilised; menstruation occurs between day 1 and days 5/6 (this is when the lining of the uterus is shed); the lining of the uterus is then built back up (to prepare for fertilised ovum); at day 14 ovulation occurs. [6 marks]

Contraception

1. a Diaphragm. [1 mark]

   b Condom. [1 mark]

   c Advantages of the plastic IUD: although the pain of periods is more severe, the pain with the copper IUD is likely to be worse; can reduce the bleeding during a period; most of the possible side effects are not serious, e.g. feeling sick, acne and headaches. [2 marks]

    Disadvantages of the plastic IUD: plastic IUD is effective for shorter period than copper IUD; has to be replaced more frequently; needs to be implanted for a period of time before it is effective, i.e. not an emergency contraception; can make the pain of periods more severe; can cause more side effects than the copper IUD; can cause some more severe side effects such as cysts on the ovaries. (Note that students should understand that the side effects are only possible and may not necessarily occur.) [2 marks]

2. Birth control pills are 99% effective in preventing pregnancy; The hormones in the pills give protection against some women's diseases; The woman's monthly periods become more regular. [3 marks]

Using hormones to treat infertility

1. FSH; LH. [2 marks]

2. Any **three** from: may increase chance of getting a sexually transmitted disease; may cause side-effects on female body; prolonged use may prevent later ovulation; may cause multiple births. [3 marks]

3. Maximum of two pros for IVM (cheaper; less hormones used; safer for the mother; IVM treatment shorter); maximum of one pro for IVF (small risk of abnormal sex chromosomes/birth defects); evaluation: (e.g. IVM better because less risk to mother outweighs small risk to baby or IVF better because no risk to baby and a small risk to mother). [4 marks]

Negative feedback

1. a Vasodilation; sweating. [2 marks]

   b Any **three** from: when temperature falls; brain detects this; sends message to muscles and glands/increase in temperature; when body temperature becomes high; brain detects and stops sending messages; negative feedback because when desired effect is reached system is turned off. [3 marks]

2. Glucose concentrations rise in the blood/glucose absorbed into blood; this stimulates the release of insulin from the pancreas/endocrine gland; insulin stimulates conversion of glucose to glycogen/insulin acts to lower blood glucose back to normal level; the lowering of glucose levels inhibits the production of insulin in a negative feedback loop. [4 marks]

Plant hormones

1. **a** In the direction of gravity. [1 mark]
   b Against force of gravity. [1 mark]
   c Diagram completed to show stem bending/leaning towards window. [1 mark]
   d More light (for leaves); more photosynthesis. [2 marks]
2. Auxin. [1 mark]
3. **a** 3. [1 mark]
   b Repeat the experiment. [1 mark]
   c Seeds germinate sooner; so growing season is longer. [2 marks]

Plant hormones and their uses

1. Gravity/geotropism; caused redistribution of auxin to lower side of stem; these hormones stimulate growth of cells on the lower side of the stem only; so the stem grows upwards. [4 marks]
2. Auxin – weedkillers; ethene – fruit ripening; gibberellins – promote flowering **and** increase fruit size. [4 marks]
3. **a** 98.67 [1 mark]
   b Control/to make sure it isn't just spraying with water that helps the plants grow taller. [1 mark]
   c The auxin caused the stems to grow much taller than those sprayed with water (98.67 cm vs 62.66 cm); therefore, the auxin caused growth of stems. [2 marks]

> **Section 6:** Inheritance, variation and evolution

Sexual reproduction and fertilisation

1. **a** Sexual reproduction. [1 mark]
   b Any **three** from: coat colour inherited/controlled by genes; It has horse and zebra features; gets gametes from both parents; genes/DNA/chromosomes/genetic information in gametes; zorse receives genes/DNA. [3 marks]
2. **a** Sexual/sex. [1 mark]
   b Egg/gamete/sex cell/ovum (reject ovule). [1 mark]

   c i Meiosis/reduction. [1 mark]
   ii Mitosis/somatic. [1 mark]
   d Any **two** from: genes/genetic information/chromosomes from two parents; alleles may be different; environmental effect/there may have been mutation. [2 marks]

Asexual reproduction

1. Parent; gamete; clone. [3 marks]
2. More/many offspring/plants (produced from one parent plant). [1 mark]
3. Requires less energy; offspring are identical to each other; produces a large number of offspring quickly; no need to find a mate. [4 marks]

Cell division by meiosis

1. Ovaries; testes. [2 marks]
2. 18 [1 mark]
3. **a** One solid and one dashed chromosome in each cell; different length chromosomes in each cell. [2 marks]
   b Nucleus. [1 mark]
   c Testes/ovaries. [1 mark]
   d Any **two** from: mitosis produces two daughter cells, meiosis produces four; mitosis produces identical daughter cells (clones), meiosis different daughter cells; mitosis diploid, meiosis haploid (must give comparison). [2 marks]

Comparing sexual and asexual reproduction

1. False; true; true; false. [4 marks]
2. Advantages: large number of identical offspring; guaranteed desired features; quick; economic. Disadvantages: may all succumb to unexpected disease/change in conditions; cut adaptation/reduce gene pool/limits variation. [5 marks]
3. Any **six** from: Plants: large numbers produced; the plants produced are identical clones; giving quicker colonisation; lack of waste, e.g. no excess pollen production; so a greater chance of survival; and no dependence on insects; water is not required for dispersal of spores/pollen grains; with adaptations to flowers to ensure transport by wind, insects or other animals.

Animals: gametes do not need to swim in liquid medium; no need to find a mate; faster than sexual reproduction; no need to waste time/energy in attracting a mate (bright feathers, courtship behaviour, etc.). [6 marks]

DNA, genes and the genome

1. Sex; genes; chromosomes; nucleus. [4 marks]

2. Chromosomes. [1 mark]

3. a Any **two** from: better preventative medicine; identify targets of drugs more effectively/ tailor healthcare/personalised medicine; search for genes linked to different types of disease; tracing human migration patterns from the past [2 marks]

   b Switching genes off and on/gene expression. [1 mark]

Structure of DNA

1. a Phosphate. [1 mark]

   b A, C, T and G. [1 mark]

   c A pairs with T; G pairs with C. [2 marks]

2. If 28% G then C must be 28%; (28 + 28 = 56)/ 100 − 56 = 44/(A + T = 44); T = 22(%). [2 marks]

3. DNA contains four bases; sequence of three bases is the code for a particular amino acid; order of bases controls the order in which amino acids are assembled; to produce a particular protein. [3 marks]

4. Hydrogen bonds; between (complementary) base pairs. [2 marks]

Protein synthesis and mutations

1. a Codon. [1 mark]

2. a CCGAUCAAC. [1 mark]

   b Three. [1 mark]

   c Ribosome. [1 mark]

3. Coding parts of DNA provide the code for sequences of amino acids/proteins; non-coding parts of DNA can switch genes on and off; both parts are affected by mutations; credit any description of mutations. [3 marks]

4. In nucleus; DNA unzips; sequence of bases in a gene act as template; to produce messenger molecule/mRNA; mRNA leaves nucleus; attaches to ribosome; carrier molecule/tRNA brings in an amino acid; complementary base pairing; tRNA attaches to ribosome;

second amino acid arrives at ribosome; amino acids attach; with peptide bond; tRNA leaves ribosome; idea that protein chain starts to grow as process is repeated; messenger molecule moves across ribosome. [4 marks]

Inherited characteristics

1. Genotype; only expressed; homozygous. [3 marks]

2. Genotype of parent A Nn; gametes N n n n; genotypes and phenotypes of young all correct. [3 marks]

3. a Gametes (B b and B b); correct combination of genotypes (BB, Bb, Bb, bb); correct analysis of phenotypes (3 black fur, 1 with brown fur). [3 marks]

   b Recognition that it is down to chance (which two gametes fuse) and not simply 'because it's a prediction' (do not accept mutation). [1 mark]

   c i B is dominant/an allele is dominant if it is expressed in the heterozygous phenotype; b is recessive/a recessive allele is not expressed in the presence of its contrasting allele. [2 marks]

      ii Alleles are different forms of a gene controlling a characteristic and occupying the same site on homologous chromosomes (e.g. B or b); genes are the units of DNA/sites on chromosomes carrying the information that determines characteristics (e.g. bB). [2 marks]

      iii Homozygous: BB/bb/possessing a pair of identical alleles for a character/true breeding. Heterozygous: Bb/carrying a pair of contrasting/different alleles for a characteristic. [2 marks]

Inherited disorders

1. a Father: Xh Y; mother: XH XH. [2 marks]

   b Phenotype: carrier; Genotype: XH Xh. [2 marks]

   c Receives normal XH from mother; Y from father. [2 marks]

   d One quarter/one out of four/25%/1:4. [1 mark]

   e Female with haemophilia must get Xh from both parents/father must have haemophilia and mother a carrier. [2 marks]

2. a Correct derivation of children's genotypes; identification of children with cystic fibrosis (dd). [2 marks]

b 0.25/25%/1:4/1 out of 4. [1 mark]

c Heterozygous. [1 mark]

3. (Mutation) changes from C to T DNA code/ there is a change in the three bases/triplet from CAG to TAG; (mutation) changes the amino acid; (this could) change the protein; (so it) forms a different shape/changed active site; (therefore) the enzyme no longer fits the substrate/carbohydrate. [5 marks]

Sex chromosomes

1. a Either of the single X boxes under 'mother'. [1 mark] **b** XY. [1 mark]

2. 50% [1 mark]

3. a 1 mark for Y in sperm box; 1 mark if XX box correct; 1 mark if both XY boxes correct. [3 marks]

b 1:1 or 50% or ½ or 0.5 or 1 in 2 or 1 out of 2 or 50:50 (do not accept 50/50). [1 mark]

Variation

1. a Differences between members of the same species/organisms of the same kind/type/ Bizzy Lizzies. [1 mark]

b Plants nearest the wall: some plants had less sun or light/more shade; less water; cooler temperature or converse (not: nutrients/ chemicals) (i.e. two from light/water/ temperature). [2 marks]

c i Environmental. [1 mark]

ii They had the same genes/DNA (or similar statement)/they are a clone. [1 mark]

2. Bacteria mutate or idea that there is variation in bacteria; leading to bacteria/resistant cells that survive antibiotic; these bacteria (resistant cells) go on to breed; do not allow bacteria get used to antibiotics or idea that antibiotics change the bacteria or bacteria become immune or references to adaptation or evolution. [3 marks]

3. a Genetics/inherited/from parent/genes/ mutation; Environment/surroundings. [2 marks]

b Any **two** from: variation caused by genetic or environmental factors; mutations causing variation in the population; large gene pool for this population, which means a large number of combinations of genes are possible. [2 marks]

Evolution by natural selection

1. Natural selection; Darwin; simple life forms. [3 marks]

2. The theory of creation does not fit with the theory of evolution. [1 mark]

3. a Lamarck. [1 mark]

b Variation/range of sword lengths (in ancestors); those with long swords get more food; swordfish (with long swords) survive **and** breed; (survivors) pass on gene(s)/allele(s) (for long sword). [4 marks]

4. Voles with a smaller body size have a higher surface area to volume ratio, which allows them to lose body heat efficiently. Smaller animals are also likely to have less body fat, which means they are less insulated/can lose heat efficiently. These better-adapted animals will survive and reproduce to pass on their beneficial genes to some of their offspring. [5 marks]

Darwin and Wallace

1. Darwin – wrote *On the Origin of Species*; Wallace – worked on warning colouration in animals; Mendel – carried out breeding experiments on pea plants. [3 marks]

2. a Natural. [1 mark]

b Three billion. [1 mark]

c Any **two** from: reference to religion; insufficient evidence; mechanism of variation/inheritance not known; reference to other theories. [2 marks]

3. Darwin's theory: parents produce more offspring than survive; there is competition among members of a species for survival/ struggle for existence; species show variation; certain variations will give a selective advantage/survival of fittest; depending on environment; these variations will be passed on to the next generation; leading to change in allele frequency. [4 marks]

Speciation

1. a 4 [1 mark]

b Ground finch/lives on the ground; (only) eats seeds. [2 marks]

2. **a** Hybridisation. [1 mark]

   b Ring species. [1 mark]

   c Genus. [1 mark]

   d Classification is based on the premise that separate species do not interbreed; these gulls are interbreeding; between species so a single classification of the species is not possible. [2 marks]

   e Any **two** from: method of obtaining oxygen through lungs; method of reproduction internal and laying eggs; homeothermic so can maintain internal temperature. [2 marks]

3. Any **six** from: a species is a group of organisms; a species shares a common gene pool; showing similar morphology/characteristics; capable of interbreeding; and producing fertile offspring; but dissimilar organisms sometimes interbreed; mule formed by crossing horse and donkey/other example of interspecific hybridisation; interspecific hybrids are sometimes fertile; sometimes organisms that are very similar will not interbreed; reference to the problem of defining fossil species; reference to the problem of species that only reproduce asexually; reference to the problem of isolated populations gradually diverging. [6 marks]

Modern understanding of genetics

1. Mendel's paper was not read widely. [1 mark]

2. **a** Factor for colour has two forms (accept allele for form); yellow dominant since all first generation yellow; green recessive since green reappears in second generation. [3 marks]

   b Genes (accept alleles) [1 mark]

   c Nucleus (accept chromosomes/DNA). [1 mark]

Fossil evidence for evolution

1. **a** Amphibians; reptiles; evolution. [3 marks]

2. **a** D [1 mark]

   b Any **two** from: hunting; collecting food; preparing food; farming; building. [2 marks]

Other evidence for evolution

1. Any **four** from: mutation produced a bird whose bill was crossed (do not allow birds decide to mutate); birds compete for food/seeds; mutant crossbill able to obtain food faster/easier/more successfully; selected for or more likely to survive; reproduce/mate/breed/produce offspring. (Maximum of 2 marks for a Lamarck explanation.) [4 marks]

2. **a** *Fusarium*. [1 mark]

   b Any **three** from: banana plants genetically identical/clones; same susceptibility/lack of resistance to Panama disease; no/little mutation; close planting enabled easy spread. [3 marks]

   c Any **six** from: natural selection; fungicide is selective agent/selective pressure; variation between individuals; chance/random mutation; some individuals have selective advantage/better chance of surviving; survival of resistants/death of non-resistants (not: survival of the fittest); mutation/ability to survive pesticide passed on to offspring; increased allele frequency. [6 marks]

3. Any **five** from: geographic distribution; ring species/other evidence from geographical distribution; biochemistry; cytochrome c/other biochemical evidence; fossils/paleontological evidence; named horse ancestor fossils; homologous structures; pentadactyl limb/vertebrate embryos/other; recent observed evolution; resistance to antibiotics/insecticides/heavy metal tolerance/other recent example. [5 marks]

4. Some bacteria not affected by antibiotic (become resistant to it); reproduce rapidly and bacteria carrying resistant genes live on to reproduce; the rapid reproduction cycle of bacteria shows how survival of the fittest leads to the selection of bacteria that are resistant and that are able to go on to produce offspring that contain their beneficial genes. [6 marks]

Extinction

1. Asteroid impact. [1 mark]

2. **a** Too cold/very cold **or** oxygen/microbes cannot reach it; for microorganisms/microbes/bacteria/fungi/enzyme/reaction to work. [2 marks]

   b No longer exist **or** no more left or died out/all died (do not credit 'died'). [1 mark]

   c Over-hunting; global warming. [2 marks]

Selective breeding

1. **a** Gamete. [1 mark] **b** Womb/uterus. [1 mark]
   c Are formed from the same original embryo.
   [1 mark] **d** Embryo transplantation [1 mark]
   e Calves will have some genes/DNA from
   bull/sperm **or** idea that sexual reproduction
   produces variation. [1 mark]

2. **a** Any **two** from: So that they do not have
   specific genetic defects; to produce docile
   cats **or** so they are not aggressive; for
   aesthetic reasons. [2 marks]

   b (Cats) are more likely to pass on (recessive)
   disorders **or** more likely to be susceptible to
   diseases. [1 mark]

   c Process: parents with the desired
   characteristic are selected; the parents
   are bred together to produce offspring;
   offspring with the desired characteristics
   are selected and bred; this is repeated over
   many generations. Explanations: parents
   who produce the least Fel D1 are initially
   selected; in their offspring there will be
   individuals with differing amounts of Fel
   D1 produced; of these, in each generation,
   the lowest Fel D1 producing individuals
   are chosen; care is taken to ensure cats
   are healthy and avoid possible problems
   associated with selective breeding; over
   time the population has increasingly low
   Fel D1-producing cats. [4 marks]

Genetic engineering

1. To produce useful substances. [1 mark]

2. Pollen from GM crops may be transported to
   neighbouring crops; herbicide-resistant crops
   may kill non-target organisms. [2 marks]

3. **a** Any **two** from: to give matching/the same
   (sticky) ends; so that the vector/plasmid
   can join with the fragment; complementary
   bases. (not: codon). [2 marks]

   b Anneals/seals/splices sticky ends together.
   [1 mark]

   c Any **three** from: reversion of virus to
   disease-causing form; bacteria/virus
   could be toxic to humans or insects; virus/
   bacterium could transfer to another species;
   accept reference to ethical reasons qualified

e.g. why change colour of leaves when there
is no nutritional value? [3 marks]

4. **a** Removal of (human) gene; plasmid is cut/
   removed from bacteria; using enzymes; gene/
   DNA (from human cell) added to plasmid;
   plasmid inserted into bacterium. [3 marks]

   b Any **one** from: to produce medicines/
   vaccines/hormones/insulin/clotting factors;
   an appropriate advantage such as e.g. cure
   diseases, for diabetes, is less likely to be
   rejected; avoids use of animals, produces large
   quantities, can be used by vegans. [1 mark]

Cloning

1. To preserve rare plant species. [1 mark]

2. Any **four** from: cells used to treat diseases
   do not go on to produce a baby; produces
   identical cells for research; cells would not
   be rejected; allow cells can form different
   types of cells; (immature) egg contains
   only genetic information/DNA/genes/
   chromosomes from mother or there is only
   one parent; asexual/no mixing of genetic
   material/no sperm involved/no fertilisation
   or chemical causes development; baby is a
   clone; reference to ethical/moral/religious
   issues. [4 marks]

3. **a** Chromosomes (allow DNA, ignore nucleus).
   [1 mark]

   b Enzymes. [1 mark]

Classification of living organisms

1. **a** Fungi. [1 mark]

   b *Russula* – genus; *silvicola* – species. [1 mark]

   c Any **two** from: photosynthesise; they feed
   autotrophically; have chlorophyll; have cell
   walls (containing cellulose); multicellular.
   [2 marks]

   d Chordata; backbone. [2 marks]

2. Any **two** from: unicellular; do not have nucleus/
   DNA in cytoplasm; circular DNA/plasmids.
   [2 marks]

3. **a** Tree. [1 mark]

   b Hippopotamus and pig. [1 mark]

   c New evidence from fossils. [1 mark]

Habitats and ecosystems

1. Photosynthesis, shelter, pollination, interdependence. [4 marks]
2. All the living organisms that interact within the same ecosystem. [1 mark]
3. Total number of one species in an ecosystem. [1 mark]
4. Labels (from top to bottom): individuals, population, community, ecosystem. [4 marks]
5. The Sun/light source provides the energy for photosynthesis; photosynthesis makes glucose and oxygen. The glucose serves as food for animals. The oxygen is used for respiration by living organisms living in the ecosystem. [4 marks]

Food in an ecosystem

1. Strawberry plant – producer; snail – primary consumer; hedgehog – secondary consumer; fox – apex predator. [4 marks]
2. An organism that makes glucose by photosynthesis. [1 mark]
3. The transfer of energy. [1 mark]
4. Snails may increase as fewer hedgehogs to eat them. Foxes may decrease as fewer hedgehogs to eat. [2 marks]

Biotic and abiotic factors

1. Pathogens; predators. [2 marks]
2. A physical condition that affects the distribution of an organism. [1 mark]
3. Any **three** from: dissolved carbon dioxide/oxygen concentration; Temperature of water; Light intensity; pH of water. [3 marks]
4. A tree removing a gas from the air. [1 mark]
5. **a** 1.5–2 m. [1 mark]
   b The distribution decreases. This might be because any higher than 2 metres it would be uncovered by sea water for too long. [2 marks]
6. The rabbit population has plenty of food so they breed and increase in number rapidly. The increase in the rabbit population means that there is more food for the fox so the fox breeds and also increases in number. There are more foxes/predators so more rabbits are eaten and the number of rabbits rapidly decreases. As the number of rabbits decreases, there is less for the fox to hunt and feed on so the number of foxes also decreases. As the numbers of foxes decreases, the fewer rabbits are eaten so more survive to breed and so the population of rabbits increases again. There is a lag between the increase of rabbits and increase of foxes because the rise of the fox population is dependent on the rise in the rabbit population. The cycle continues. [6 marks]

Adapting for survival

1. Camel – large surface area to volume ratio; polar bear – thick fur and blubber; toad – long sticky tongue. [3 marks]
2. Structural adaptations are physical features of an organism. Behavioural adaptations are the things organisms do to survive. [2 marks]
3. The stings deter herbivores from eating the nettles. [1 mark]
4. Extremophiles. [1 mark]
5. Large ears: have big surface area and can be flapped to cool down. Tusks: for digging into ground to search for food or water. [2 marks]

Measuring population size and species distribution

1. Place a tape measure 20 m across the trampled area to form a transect line. Place the 1 m² quadrat against the transect line so that one corner of it touches the 0 m mark on the tape measure. Count and record the number of buttercups within the quadrat. Repeat this process at 5-metre intervals along the transect line. Repeat this process at the untrampled area. [5 marks]
2. **a** Mean: 8 ÷ 5 = 1.6; mode: 0; median: 1. [3 marks]
   b Fewer buttercups due to less light/water in soil. [2 marks]

Cycling materials

1. Carbon; nitrogen; cylced; physical. [2 marks]

Answers

2. **a** Photosynthesis. [1 mark]

   b Respiration; combustion. [2 marks]

   c They return carbon dioxide back to the atmosphere when they respire. [1 mark]

   d Bacteria and fungi need oxygen to respire and produce energy when decomposing the organic material. [1 mark] Waterlogged soils do not have much oxygen so the decomposers have less energy and work more slowly. [1 mark]

3. $7.4 - 5.3 = 2.1$; $2.1/5.3 \times 100 = 39.62\%$ [2 marks]

4. Every living organism on Earth depends on water to survive. Without water and the water cycle to circulate water, all living organisms would die very quickly. It is needed for chemical reactions in living organisms such as respiration and photosynthesis. [3 marks]

Decomposition

1. Digest; recycle; fungi; enzymes. [2 marks]

2. Extremes of pH slow down the reproduction of decomposers and can kill them. [1 mark]

3. Low temperatures slow the rate of reaction of enzymes and will prevent growth and reproduction of microorganisms. [2 marks]

4. Biogas is produced naturally in marshes, septic tanks and sewers. Biogas generators provide a cheaper fuel source. [2 marks]

5. **a** When the fat in the milk is broken down by the lipase, fatty acids are made. The fatty acids lower the pH of the mixture causing the colour change. [2 marks]

   b Increasing the temperature increases the rate of reaction by increasing the collision rate between the enzyme and substrate molecules. This means the enzyme-controlled reactions that cause decay are increased and the rate of decay of milk increases up until 45°C. After 45°C the rate of enzyme reactions decreases as temperature increases until, at some point, the reaction stops altogether. The protein structure of the enzyme is denatured by temperatures above 40°C causing the molecule to lose its shape which deactivates the enzyme. As a result, the enzyme-controlled reactions that cause decay cannot occur. [4 marks]

Changing the environment

1. Sinking of land bridge joining two contin animals cannot move between continents; Low temperatures and food shortage – animals hibernate longer than normal; Global warming causes sea to become more acidic – shells of calcareous organisms dissolve and become thinner. [3 marks]

2. Higher average temperatures caused by sunspot activity. Increased atmospheric carbon dioxide and sulfur dioxide due to volcanic activity. [2 marks]

3. Increase in salinity: species not tolerant to change in salt would decrease/proliferation of species adapted to survive in more saline environments. Decrease in oxygen: decease in marine life due to less oxygen concentration. Decrease in decomposition if insufficient oxygen for decomposers and therefore buildup of remains of dead plants and animals. Increase in sea temperature: species not tolerant to higher temperatures would die/increase in species better adapted to warmer sea temperature. [3 marks]

Effects of human activities

1. All the variety of all the different species of organisms on earth or within an ecosystem. [1 mark]

2. Biodiversity ensures the stability of ecosystems by reducing the dependence of one species on another for food, territory or mates. [1 mark]

3. There is less food available for insect pollinators such as bees. Habitats are destroyed. [2 marks]

4. To produce garden compost. [1 mark]

5. To provide land for cattle or rice fields for food. To grow biofuel crops. [2 marks]

6. **a** $100 - 65 - 3 = 32\%$. [1 mark]

   b 1. Habitats may be destroyed by landfill site; 2. Toxic chemicals from landfill can pollute land and water. [2 marks]

7. Any **four** from: burning of trees releases carbon dioxide into the atmosphere; microorganisms that breakdown remaining plant material also produce carbon dioxide as they respire; fewer trees means less photosynthesis so less carbon dioxide removed from atmosphere; less biodiversity as fewer habitats; more erosion of soil and landslides; less transpiration of water from trees can impact microclimate. [4 marks]

Global warming

1. Carbon dioxide and methane. [2 marks]
2. Any **two** from: burning fossil fuels; more rice crops; increase in cattle farming; deforestation; destruction of peatlands; more petrol cars being used; any other appropriate answer. [2 marks]
3. The graph shows that the temperature has fluctuated but there is an overall increase in global temperature. The graph clearly shows an overall trend of increasing global temperatures/ an increase of 0.7 degrees between 1880 and 2000. This is strong evidence that global warming is happening as the temperature increase is more in recent years compared with 1880. Overall, the evidence for global warming shown by the graph is quite strong. [4 marks]
4. Any **four** from: Rise in sea level due to ice caps and glaciers melting, so loss of habitat from flooding; change in distribution of species in areas where rainfall/temperature changes. Some species might increase if they favour new conditions, but others are likely to become endangered by unfavourable conditions; changes to migration patterns; loss of wetland in the African Sahel; would cause turtles and birds to decrease in numbers and possibly become extinct. [4 marks]

Maintaining biodiversity

1. By replanting hedgerows. [1 mark]
2. Any **two** from: they provide a habitat for a wide range of plants and animals, e.g. wildflowers, insects and birds; provide wildlife corridors, allowing wildlife to move freely between habitats to find food, shelter, mates; wildflowers are important sources of nectar and pollen for insect-pollinators so field margins promote the pollination of plant species dependent on insect-pollinators. [2 marks]
3. Less waste goes to landfill so fewer habitats destroyed by landfill sites and less land, water and air pollution associated with landfill; materials are recycled so fewer trees need to be used to make new paper; less pollution associated with manufacturing paper from wood. [3 marks]
4. Planting trees does result in more carbon dioxide being absorbed from the atmosphere during photosynthesis. Carbon dioxide emissions from human activities are high so a huge number of trees would need to be planted to offset carbon dioxide emissions. [2 marks]

5. They keep damage to food chains and food webs to a minimum. They can attract tourists and therefore benefit the economy. [2 marks]
6. Any **two** points from: local people might rely on the mangrove forests for food so might not want it to be protected; local people or building companies might not know about the importance of the mangrove so might think it doesn't matter if it gets destroyed; mangroves are complicated ecosystems that require the involvement of experts for restoration, and finding experts may be difficult/expensive. [2 marks]

Biomass in an ecosystem

1. Mass; dry; energy. [4 marks]
2. 1 mark for calculating correct biomass at each level: Level 1 = 200; level 2 = 20; level 3 = 5. 1 mark for drawing pyramid in correct order and labelling correctly. 1 mark for drawing levels to scale.
3. Losses of biomass are due to: not all the ingested material being absorbed, some is egested as faeces; [1 mark] some absorbed material is lost as waste, e.g. carbon dioxide and water in respiration, urea in urine; [1 mark] large amounts of glucose are used in respiration. [1 mark]
4. $7900/80000 \times 100$; [1 mark] = 9.9%. [1 mark]

Food security

1. Having enough food to feed a population. [1 mark]
2. Increasing birth rate; new pests that affect farming; Increasing costs of pesticides. [3 marks]
3. Drought would result in lower crop yield due to less water for plants, less photosynthesis able to take place and less crop growth. [2 marks]
4. Meeting the needs of the current population without affecting the ability of future generations to meet their needs. [1 mark]
5. Any **two** from: buying from sustainable fishery; fishing quotas; control of net size; high-protein fish food. [2 marks]
6. Advantage: restricted movement of chickens means they use less energy for movement and more can be used for growth so shorter time needed to achieve slaughter weight and improved production/higher economical yields. Disadvantage: close confinement often causes suffering to chickens by increased risk of disease/lack of movement, lack of natural light/ unable to express natural behaviours. [2 marks]

Answers

Role of biotechnology

1. Living; increasing; sustainable; nutritious. [2 marks]
2. It can help prevent night blindness caused by vitamin A deficiency. [1 mark]
3.

Level 3: The response considers most of the advantages and disadvantages, and gives an opinion about use of biotechnology to produce insulin based on the points raised. The response is well structured.	5–6
Level 2: The response considers some of the advantages and disadvantages, and gives an opinion about use of biotechnology to produce insulin based on the points raised. The response has some structure.	4–5
Level 1: The response considers at least one advantage and one disadvantage. There may be an attempt at a concluding opinion but it may not be supported by the points raised. The response may lack structure.	1–2

Indicative content

Advantages:

- Human insulin can be produced in large quantities.
- The process is not time-consuming and is inexpensive compared to previous methods.
- The insulin is indistinguishable from human insulin produced in the pancreas, and therefore is less likely to cause allergic reactions in people with diabetes.
- The insulin is produced in a very controlled and sterile environment and then purified to ensure the insulin is pure and of the required quality.
- The insulin is absorbed more rapidly than animal-derived insulin and acts faster.

Disadvantages:

- The production costs are still high.
- Some people think that genetic engineering is not ethical.